GREATER MANCHESTER IN 1998 - 1999

A REVIEW OF ORGANISATIONS, TRANSPORT OPERATORS AND THEIR TICKET AND FARE COLLECTION SYSTEMS

PAUL J SMITH

AND

BRIAN HUGHES

The Transport Ticket Society

1999

Comments etc. regarding this publication are welcome; please write to the Society's Publications Officer:

David Harman
24 Frankfield Rise
Tunbridge Wells
TN2 5LF

E-Mail: David.Harman@btinternet.com

Front cover: Manchester Piccadilly Gardens from the top floor of the Greater Manchester PTE building, showing buses of the three main groups and Metrolink trams. July 1999.

Rear cover: The restored frontage of Manchester Victoria Station with the Metrolink overhead wiring just visible through the entrance archway. July 1999.

[both: Brian Hughes]

ISBN 0 903209 32 2

Published by
The Transport Ticket Society
81 Pilgrims Way, Kemsing, Sevenoaks, TN15 6TD

Printed by
Paterson Printing Ltd,
Tunbridge Wells

Introduction

This publication looks at organisations and operators that issued tickets for travel within "Greater Manchester" during the period April 1998 through March 1999 - so far as they are known to the authors. Events that have taken place since 31 March 1999 are not covered in this volume.

The impetus for the production of this publication came from an appeal at the 1998 Annual General Meeting of The Transport Ticket Society for members to follow up Brian Pask's successful publication "London in 1997" with similar books on their own local areas. No initial keenness was exhibited by the present authors to produce such a volume for Greater Manchester, but the period under consideration they found so interesting, that by the end of 1998 they had reached a tacit agreement with one another to "have a go". The authors are indebted to the very many individuals and companies within Greater Manchester who have been so generous with their time when searching points of clarification were fired at them! Without some of the information thus obtained, this volume would have been far less comprehensive in coverage and a little less accurate in detail.

Brian Hughes
Paul Smith
July 1999

Index

1   Background

It is relevant that we first of all clarify the geography of the area being considered - namely the "old" metropolitan county of Greater Manchester. This now comprises the ten unitary metropolitan districts of Bolton, Bury, Manchester, Oldham, Rochdale, Salford, Stockport, Tameside, Trafford and Wigan. The Local Government Act of 1985 allowed for the establishment of a **Passenger Transport Authority** in Greater Manchester. This is primarily a policy making body with responsibility for assessing the public transport needs of the area, and is a joint board comprising thirty elected representatives drawn from these ten metropolitan districts.

GMPTA provides financial support for

- non-commercial bus services in Greater Manchester.
- some local rail services.
- concessionary support for the elderly, children and certain categories of disabled people.
- accessible transport services for mobility impaired people
- provision of bus stations, shelters and stops.

- public information and the general promotion of passenger transport.
- the development of the rail network.

2   Greater Manchester Passenger Transport Executive

The funding for supporting the PTA's activities comes from each of the ten District Councils, and the Greater Manchester Passenger Transport Executive carries out all of these duties on behalf of the Authority.

The Passenger Transport Executive implements the policies of the Passenger Transport Authority by

- monitoring the county's bus network and in accordance with Authority policy, where necessary, invites tenders for bus services not provided commercially [which includes most of the school bus services].
- monitoring Greater Manchester's local rail network to ensure that local train services meet local needs.
- providing the operating infrastructure: i.e. bus stations, passenger shelters, bus stops and service terminal points (turn-rounds) for the use of all bus operators and their passengers.
- administering the Free and Concessionary Fares Scheme
- implementing policies which reflect the Authority's commitment to improving the accessibility of public transport services for all potential users, including the provision of special services (including the Ring & Ride door to door service, special ticketing - such as Travel Vouchers for use in taxis - and the provision of grants to operators to upgrade their fleets with vehicles that have low floor access).
- providing information about, and promoting public transport in Greater Manchester
- providing, so far as is practicable, reasonable integration of bus/rail services through the promotion and administration of a County-wide off bus ticket sales scheme.
- developing and promoting Metrolink, Manchester's light rapid transit system (which the PTE owns).
- collecting information about the use of public transport and needs of its users and in line with the Authority's policies planning for the future of public transport in both specific and general terms (including bus priority schemes, park and ride initiatives).

Concessionary Travel
The Passenger Transport Executive administers a scheme that gives cheaper travel to children, students, pensioners and mobility-impaired people, and sets the level of the Countywide Concessionary fare. This was 34p per journey until 14 November and 36p thereafter.

Passengers eligible for travel at concessionary rates are:

- children under 16. (Children aged under 13 do not need a pass or proof of age. Children aged 13 to 15 inclusive are encouraged to carry an UNDER 16 proof of age card: styled "ID -16").
- Senior Citizens resident within the ten Districts (on production of a valid Permit).
- people whose ability to walk is seriously impaired (at the discretion of the District Councils and on production of a valid Permit)
- full time students in further education (not higher education) aged between 16 and 19 years, resident in Greater Manchester, travelling to and from college (on production of a valid Permit).

Certain members of the public resident within Greater Manchester are entitled to free travel on buses. These include:

- under 5's (no Pass or proof of age required).
- blind people (on production of a valid Pass).
- profoundly deaf people who are also without speech (on production of a valid Pass).

- limb-less ex-service personnel with specific arm and leg disabilities resulting from their military service (on production of a valid Pass).
- mentally impaired people (on production of a valid Pass).

All of the current Passes and Permits feature a "corporate design" with the GMPTE "M" logo in a coloured stripe towards the left-hand edge, and "GMPTE" printed towards the bottom of this stripe. Various security devices are used on the Passes and Permits in an attempt to prevent fraudulent usage, including a laminated cover, a photograph of the authorised holder, holographic features and a security background of varying colour intensity.

All Free Passes have a yellow background, whilst Concessionary Permits have a white background. Text colour on Free Travel Passes/Permits for the disabled is always brown; on Passes/Permits issued on an annual basis the text colour is varied in rotation: blue, green, brown, purple, red. 1997/8 issues were brown; 1998/9 issues were purple, whilst 1999/2000 issues are blue.

The following Passes and Permits are issued by the PTE:

- **Disabled Persons Concessionary Permit**: issued annually to women 16-59 and men 16-64 and whose ability to walk is seriously impaired. Decisions regarding eligibility for this Permit lies with the Local Social Services Department. Features a red corporate stripe, hologrammed "Permit" and "Concessionary" in gradation of colour (which varies in rotation as given above).
- **Disabled Persons Free Travel Pass**: issued to disabled, blind, profoundly deaf, limbless ex-service personnel etc. These invariably feature a brown corporate stripe and brown text ("Free Travel") in gradation of colour on a yellow background. There are issues with expiry dates for every month (except September) each year as they are renewed upon expiry on a month by month basis. Persons suffering from a short-term condition are issued with Passes expiring after one year; those with longer-term conditions are issued with Passes expiring after three years.
- **Senior Citizen Concessionary Travel Permit** (also known as "Bus Pass"). These are issued for life. An example is shown in the section of coloured illustrations. As will be noted, the corporate stripe is red on which is a hologrammed "Life". The word "Concessionary" is in gradation of colour (blue). [As the design of this Permit has changed over time (and was previously styled "Pensioners Permit"), older styles could be encountered during our survey period.]
- **Scholar Concessionary Travel Permit** (to/from school/college). Corporate stripe in red and including hologrammed "Scholar". "Concessionary" in gradation of colour: Valid until 31 July 98 - purple; valid until July 99 - red (in line with colour rotation sequence given above).
- **Scholar Free Travel Pass** (to/from school/college). Yellow background, corporate stripe in red plus hologrammed "Scholar". "Free" in gradation of colour (sequence as above).
- **Journey Variance Vouchers**. (The two scholar passes/permits are only valid up until 6.00pm Monday - Friday. Their availability at other times in connection with bona fide school activities is extended if the permit holder has one of these vouchers giving details of the out of hours usage. Current vouchers, in the PTE "corporate style" have a white background, corporate stripe in grey and a security background with repeats of "JOURNEY VARIANCE VOUCHER" in blue.

- **ID-16** (Under Sixteen identity card). A card that proves that the holder is entitled to travel at the current Concessionary fare within the area of validity in Greater Manchester. The date shown is the day before the holder's sixteenth birthday. These have a shaded red/blue/red background, a corporate stripe in navy and a hologrammed "ID-16".

A reciprocal agreement with West Yorkshire in respect of concessionary travel was in force during the survey year. Greater Manchester Disabled Persons Free Pass/ Concessionary Permit holders and Senior Citizens Concessionary Permit holders travelling in West Yorkshire paid full fare before 0930 Monday - Friday; the West Yorkshire Concessionary fare (20p) from 0930 until 1500 and after 1800 Monday - Friday; and half adult fare 1500 - 1800 Monday - Friday. At weekends and on public holidays, the West Yorkshire Concessionary fare was payable. No reciprocal agreements were in force with any other neighbouring counties, but some amelioration of fare payable was in force in respect of cross boundary journeys: half the total adult fare for the entire journey (Concessionary Permit holders); half fare from the county boundary (Free Pass holders). Scholars Pass/Permit holders were not entitled to any allowance on journeys outwith Greater Manchester.

Travel Vouchers are a relatively new form of travel concession. They were first introduced on a trial basis in Wigan and Bolton during the financial year 1994-95, and extended to become a county-wide scheme the following year (the trial having proved successful). The vouchers are available to people resident in Greater Manchester who are

1. registered as blind with their local authority
2. in receipt of Disability Living Allowance Higher Rate for Mobility or 24 Hour Attendance Allowance or War Pensions Mobility supplement
3. unable to walk 400 metres or more or climb steps of 300mm or more (and certified by a doctor)

Vouchers are valid for travel by any taxi owned by taxi companies registered to participate in the scheme or on accessible (low floor) bus services, Ring & Ride and Community Transport.

In 1998/99, the vouchers come in booklets of 15, costing £5: each voucher being valued at £1. Each user was entitled to have up to £90 worth of vouchers in the year at a cost of £30 (the year corresponded to our survey period i.e. from 1 April to 31 March).

Qualifying individuals wishing to join the Travel voucher scheme have first to surrender their Free Travel Pass or Concessionary Travel Permit. In exchange they receive a Travel Voucher User Card which has a green background, corporate stripe in dark green and wording "Travel Vouchers" in black.

The travel vouchers valid for 1998/99 were coloured pale blue (including the corporate stripe) on a white background. Note that the colour of these changes annually, but not in the sequence given for other Concessionary Passes/Permits.

[As an aside, it is probably appropriate to record here that the PTE views favourably those schools within Greater Manchester that co-operate proactively to reduce misbehaviour by pupils on services to/from schools that they have financially supported. Many schools have therefore introduced their own photo-identity cards. An example that the writers are able to illustrate comes from The Deane School in Bolton, which was served by route 912 during the survey period. The card is encapsulated in a heavy-duty clear plastic laminate.]

Wayfarer (multi-modal, cross-boundary tickets)

Greater Manchester PTE also promotes a range of multi-modal, cross-boundary cards under this name, and at the beginning of April 1998 the scheme had a major revamp when - for the first time - travel throughout the Metrolink network after 0930 and all day at weekends and Bank Holidays was added. (Previously, only travel within the Metrolink City Zone had been included in the validity). At this time, there was no change to bus and rail validity.

The previous style of ticket was replaced on 6 April with a new three-part form, comprising on the front looking from left to right:

- The ticket, with scratch off panels, including years 1998/1999/2000/2001 on the front and seven Conditions of Use on the back (but no map);
- A travel survey, with 2nd class business reply service postage
- An opportunity to win a £25 Marks & Spencer Gift Voucher (if the survey/card is fully completed!)

Prices for the various types of Wayfarer ticket became £6.60 Adult, £3.30 Concession, £11.00 Group, and £10.00 Weekend. Ticket colours are orange, blue, green and pink respectively: all with a navy stripe at the top containing the GMPTE logo. The Concession ticket was new, having replaced the previously separate Child and Senior Citizen issues. As a consequence, the price paid by Senior Citizens for a Wayfarer ticket decreased from £3.50.

The previous style of Wayfarer ticket remained valid after 6 April, but validity of such tickets continued to be restricted in respect of travel on Metrolink. However, holders of these tickets could exchange them or receive a refund by returning them to the PTE. The upgrade was free - even where there had been an increase in the price.

It should be noted that there had been new issues of the Child and Senior Citizen cards (and possibly others) from 1 January 1998, and carrying year scratch off panels 1998/1999/2000 - making them especially short-lived varieties.

The publicity leaflet announcing the new tickets included a McDonalds promotion: a cut out voucher valid until 21 March 1999. New leaflets covering the subsequent twelve months (22 March 1999 - 2 April 2000) were then produced and these also included a new McDonald's promotional offer.

Wayfarer tickets are excellent value for anyone travelling widely during the course of a day, as the geographical area extends well beyond Greater Manchester into the Peak District and also parts of West Yorkshire (e.g. to Holmfirth and Todmorden), Lancashire (e.g. to Burnley, Accrington and Chorley), Cheshire (e.g. to Warrington, Northwich and Congleton) and Staffordshire (e.g. Biddulph and Leek). It is also possible to reach Sheffield (but only on service X23 [but shown as X18 on the new 1999 leaflet]!).

Wayfarer tickets are accepted on *most* bus services within this area at any time. Travel by train and Metrolink is only permitted after 0930 Mondays to Fridays, but is unrestricted at weekends and on Bank Holidays.

Conference TravelCard

The PTE also has these tickets available for issue, if required. They were originally produced for a specific major conference a few years ago and have remained in stock ever since. Whilst they remain available, the facility has not been overtly marketed for a while. The card features a complex tri-folding design (measuring 148 x 207mm) with a grey corporate stripe and a mottled light blue background. Text is printed in a variety of colours. The other side of the card features two maps: the first showing the boundaries of bus validity, the second showing the train and Metrolink stations to which it may be used. Between these is a statement of the validity of the TravelCard.

Rouletted to the middle section of the card thus described is the Conference TravelCard itself (see illustration) including inclusive validity dates, serial number and a statement of Validity. On the back are eight terms and conditions and a space for the conference delegate to sign the card. A print code (13830-893-2000) is shown, suggesting that the cards were produced in August 1993.

Piccadilly Travel Shop: Rail Ticket Agency
The PTE's travel shop located at Piccadilly Plaza, Manchester (adjacent to Piccadilly Bus Station), is licensed to sell railway tickets. The travel shop is not equipped with APTIS or TRIBUTE equipment for ticket issue. Use is therefore made of booklet tickets, onto which travel details, reservations etc. must be hand-written. The writers have not seen examples of issued tickets from this outlet.

ID-16 Card

Journey Variance Voucher

ID-16 Card image with Name, Valid until, GMPTE, UNDER SIXTEEN, CA 102766, EP 2001

School Journey Variance Voucher

Deane School Photo-ID

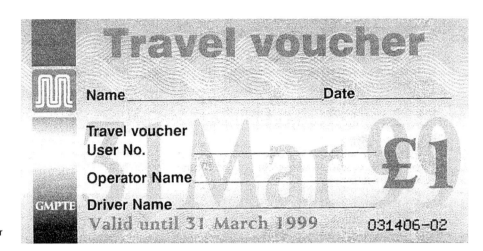

Taxi Travel Voucher

Promotional card for a taxi company
accepting GMPTE Travel Vouchers

Integrate Scheme Day Saver

Conference
Travel Card

3   System 1 Travel

System 1 Travel is the marketing name of **Greater Manchester Travelcards Ltd (GMTL)**. Originally based at Portland Tower (53 Portland Street, Manchester), GMTL moved to 3 Horsedge Street, Oldham during 1998.

The company - essentially a "marketing and distribution club" and owned jointly by the constituent bus operators and Greater Manchester PTE - came into existence on 1 January 1994. It replaced the Inter Operators' Ticketing Association (IOTA) that had itself been formed in 1988 to promote a range of tickets eventually introduced in 1991 as replacement for the PTEs "Saver" range. The new range of cards although administered by the PTE was basically an operators' scheme. In 1993 it was widely felt that the existing arrangement needed to be formalised, and during the course of that year the basis for a company was developed and a joint venture agreement formulated. This outlined the inter-operator responsibilities and established the rules for running the company including the method of revenue distribution (and including the basis for assimilating new members) and the establishment of indemnities.

This company might have fallen foul of the Office of Fair Trading (OFT), but the OFT gave its blessing to the formation of GMTL because

- revenue was to be distributed according to market share
- constituent operators were still free to have their own day/period ticket schemes
- it was open to all-comers, including new operators

All of the 50 bus operators with services within Greater Manchester signed up to the new agreement in December 1993. A Board of ten directors was originally established to oversee the workings of GMTL. There were two directors each from the companies now known as Stagecoach Manchester and First Manchester; the group of "medium-sized operators" elected four directors (during the survey period these were from Arriva Manchester Ltd., A Mayne & Sons Ltd., Rossendale Transport Ltd. and Bluebird Bus & Coach.); whilst the group of "small operators" elected one director (M Bull from Bu-Val during the survey period) and with the final place being allocated to the PTE representative.

It will be noted that Metrolink and the Train operators were not originally members. GMPTE represented their interests at Board meetings. When the Section 22 agreement finished with the Train Operating Companies (TOCs), GMTL itself entered into operational agreements with North West Trains (now First North Western) and the other TOCs. At the time of writing, First North Western was in the process of applying to become a member of GMTL, and once admitted will have a director on the Board. Altram (the owners of the Metrolink network) became a fully-fledged member of GMTL at the time of the launch of the "Integrate" day tickets (see below), and that company's MD now sits on the GMTL Board.

New System 1 Travelcards, valid with an appropriate Club Card (16-19 or Adult), replaced the existing range of Travelcards from Monday 5 February 1996. These continued unchanged during the period covered by this survey, comprising:

- **Adult Bus Saver**: 7 day, 1 month, Annual [pale/dark orange, pale/dark burgundy and pale blue/navy respectively] (N.B. the Annual ticket is only available by postal application to the PTE)
- **Adult Buscard Extra**: 7 day, 1 month (available as an "add-on" for holders of a Rail Season ticket or Metrolink Period Pass) [pale/dark green, pale/dark pink respectively]

- **Junior Bus Saver**: 7 day only
- **16 - 19 Bus Saver**: 7 day only and including a special issue with "RE" prefix to the serial numbers, for Rochdale Training & Enterprise Council (now part of Rochdale Borough Chamber)
- **County Bus & Train Saver**: 7 day, 1 month, Annual [green/dark green, pale blue/royal blue and Rail Season Ticket respectively] (N.B. the Annual ticket is only available from main rail outlets; previously there was a System 1 card issued for this facility)

In addition, there are two tickets only available to passengers entitled to travel concessions:

- **Concessionary Clippercard**: available to anyone qualifying for GMPTE concessionary travel (i.e. children, senior citizens permit holders and mobility impaired permit holders) and providing ten any distance **bus** journeys for approximately the price of nine. [Many of the buses of the "major" operators were generally equipped with Almex M (top) cancellors during the survey period to decrement these tickets. However, smaller operators had supplied their drivers with hand cancellors. During 1998, however, a number of operators fitted new cancellation devices for driver usage: either on the ticket machine, or adjacent to this.]
- **Senior Day Card**: available for use by those in possession of a valid GMPTE concessionary pass, these are scratch off tickets available either singly (this is a relatively new provision) or in packs (previously books) of five, each one valid for one day on unlimited bus journeys throughout Greater Manchester.

During the period under consideration, the Concessionary Clippercard passed through serials suffixed B and C, and these cards continued to show the Portland Street address. Although the leaflet promoting the System 1 range of Travelcards features an illustration of a System 1 Senior Day Card with scratch-off years 1995/1996/1997/1998/1999 (as indeed does the illustration used on the internet site), no such card has yet been seen, so great were the stocks of the former PTE print (with the same printed dates).

The existence of GMTL with its unique identifying logo, along with its benchmark "all for one - one for all" philosophy has had a major impact on the Quality Partnership issue which is at the forefront of public transport developments - and particularly local transport planning - at the moment. The expediency of a range of different operators working together is already in place in Greater Manchester and allowed for a major new ticketing initiative to be more easily established.

This major new initiative and marketed by System 1 Travel commenced from 27 September 1998. Under the "**Greater Manchester Integrate**" transport strategy initiative (which is supported by GMPTA, GMPTE, the Association of Greater Manchester Authorities, the Highways Agency, the Greater Manchester Bus Owners Association (nearly all the bus operators), First North Western Trains, Railtrack, Altram, Manchester Airport and Greater Manchester Travelcards Ltd.) a new range of Daysaver tickets was introduced and comprising:

- Bus Only (£3.00 for unlimited travel all day)
- Bus & Train (£3.50 for unlimited travel after 0930, all day Saturday, Sunday, Bank Holidays)
- Bus & Metrolink (£5.00 - available as above)
- Bus, Train & Metrolink (£7.00 - available as above)

There were no special cards for these tickets, each bus

operator issuing one of their normal machine tickets at the appropriate fare. Illustrated is a Bus Only ticket issued on Blackburn Transport Service 702. The first time one of the authors attempted to purchase such a ticket on this service, the driver said that he was unable to issue one. It is understood that the driver concerned was later made aware of the appropriate procedure to issue a Day Saver ticket and also received a short revision course on "customer care"! Initially the tickets could not be issued by Arriva Midlands North, Bellairs & Dootson, First Calderline, First Kingfisher, Trent Buses or MTL or on school contract service buses - though the tickets could be used on these services.

Metrolink ticket vending machines at Metrolink stations were modified to issue the tickets that included Metrolink availability by using two of the buttons that had previously been used for city centre destinations, and normal ticket stock was used for these tickets. (By 15 February 1999, the TVMs had issued 344 bus + Metrolink and 12 bus + train + Metrolink tickets!)

The tickets that included rail availability were obtainable from staffed railway stations in Greater Manchester and rail tickets showed destination TRAVELCARD TB or TRAVELCARD TBM and from APTIS were supposed to be issued on One Day Rover/One Day Ranger 4599/5 stock. Tickets were also available from on-train conductors, and SPORTIS issues should show destination TRAVELCARD* and Ticket Type as DAY RANGER or DAY ROVER.

Looking to the future, there are three likely areas upon which GMTL may focus developments:

- the pricing structure and operation of the County Card in order to make purchase more attractive for more customers;
- a greater involvement of Metrolink in multi-operator tickets (i.e. extension of the present range to include period tickets);
- the introduction of contactless smartcards (which has an implication for the ticket-issuing equipment that operators will need to have in order to be able to provide an effective interface for customers making use of smartcards)

Appendix 1 shows the Bus Operator members of GMTL as at 3 November 1998. We are indebted to Jim Hulme of GMTL for this information.

Concessionary Clippercard

Adult Club Card issued to one of the authors of this publication

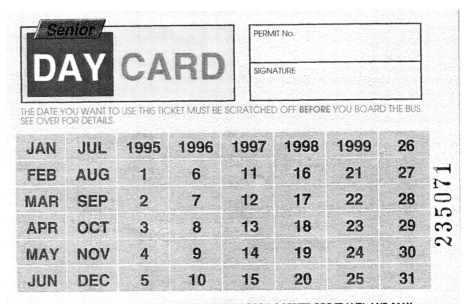

Senior Day Buscard

4   Skyline

This is the brand name for a quality partnership initiative covering the most frequent bus services operating to/from Manchester Airport. It was officially launched on 30 September 1998. Under this branding, it is the intention "to co-ordinate schedules, improve the flexibility of ticketing, provide passengers with greater choice and enhance the appeal of bus services to/from Manchester Airport", according to publicity material.

Three bus companies have combined to provide the Skyline network: Stagecoach Manchester, Arriva Manchester and Trent. Many of the vehicles used on the Skyline services are new and came complete with special Skyline livery or have been repainted into this livery.

From inception through to the end of the survey period, all of the Skyline services served the Airport bus station, adjacent to Terminal 1. However, some also served other parts of the airport (e.g. the railway station [with pedestrian connections for Terminal 2 and the Airport Job Centre], Olympic House [with pedestrian connection for Terminal 1 British Airways - but restyled Terminal 3 from 28 March 1999] and the World Freight Terminal).

Special Weekly and Monthly Skyliner tickets were introduced from the launch of Skyline for Manchester Airport employees and costing £9 and £36 respectively and which are valid for unlimited travel on any Skyline route and many other Stagecoach Manchester, Arriva Manchester and Trent services in south Manchester. The tickets are essentially aimed at those airport employees who need to change buses to/from the airport and in particular where travel is of necessity by more than one operator. [Note that validity of the tickets actually covers 8 days and a calendar month plus one day respectively, which allows travel in to the airport on the day after expiry would otherwise have happened.]

The tickets are laminated cards, into which are inserted a Wayfarer 3 machine-issue. These are obtained from the Thomas Cook outlet in T1 Arrivals. Arriva Manchester has supplied a ticket machine to issue the tickets, and this company is also responsible for processing the revenue distribution amongst the three companies following analysis of statistics downloaded from the ticket machine module. Airport employees have to give their postcode when they purchase a ticket, and the agreed revenue distribution is derived from this postcode data.

Tickets have to be presented with the employee's Airport ID pass, and the ID number and a signature have to be entered onto the right-hand end of the ticket before lamination. The back of one of these tickets is illustrated. The text on the front appears to have been at least partly derived from Trent's Day Explorer Ticket, because this includes "'This peel and seal wallet will keep your ticket secure for the day" and "Enjoy your day!" This is, of course, hidden once the validating Wayfarer ticket has been inserted. However, the card also states "7 days travel for Manchester Airport employees" along the top edge - and this same version is being issued for the monthly tickets. Text on the front is in blue on white, whilst the reverse (illustrated) is multi-coloured.

Modifications to the ticket are planned when a reprint is needed (this was not imminent on 31 March 1999) and discussions were also underway at that time with a view to introducing a multi-journey ClipperCard type ticket (probably for 12 -journeys) that would be appropriate for employees with a less regular working pattern.

Each operator's own Weekly/7-day tickets are also available for airport employees of course, purchased on the bus.

Reverse of Skyliner laminate

5   First Manchester Ltd

This company, with headquarters in Oldham and operational bases additionally at Wigan, Bolton, Bury and Queens Road, Manchester is one of the two major operators in Greater Manchester with its origins in Greater Manchester Transport, the operational bus company of Greater Manchester PTE. In 1986, Greater Manchester Buses Ltd. was formed to comply with the requirements of The Transport Act 1985, whereby all Local Authority bus undertakings had to be transferred into limited company operations by 26 October 1986 (the date on which bus services in England, Scotland and Wales were deregulated - another major provision of the 1985 Act).

The Government required that Local Authority-owned bus companies should be privatised, and this was not something that was actively sought by Greater Manchester Buses Ltd or its local authority owners. However, in April 1993, the Greater Manchester PTA announced that G M Buses would be split into two companies (Greater Manchester Buses North Ltd and Greater Manchester Buses South Ltd) to meet government pressure for its break-up and sale. Although this division into two was originally planned for June 1993, it was not until September of that year that this actually took place. In February 1994, The GMPTA announced that it was accepting an employee buyout bid of £27 million for Greater Manchester Buses North Ltd in the face of two competing bids. The sale was completed in March of that year. Less than three years later, in February 1997, the company was re-sold and became part of the rapidly expanding FirstBus empire. In early 1998, because of the increasing diversity of the "First" brand, the empire was renamed "FirstGroup" and Greater Manchester Buses North Ltd was renamed First Manchester Ltd from 6 May 1998.

Wayfarer ticket machines/rolls

On-vehicle ticketing utilised Wayfarer II ticket equipment throughout the period under consideration. Definitive Wayfarer rolls, white and with "Greater Manchester *f*" in red began to be replaced by similar tickets but titled "First Manchester" by early June 1998. (Inconsistent usage of stocks meant that earlier blue-printed "Greater Manchester *f*" rolls saw occasional use during the period under consideration, and the red-printed version with this title had not reached complete extinction!)

Quite a selection of promotional Wayfarer rolls saw usage over the 12-month period (First Manchester title unless indicated with "*"):
- Kellogg's Nutri-Grain
- KFC (Bolton, 2 outlets + Wigan: until 18.05.98.; advertiser's logo on front)
- Littlewoods Restaurant (two separate rolls [both *]: until 30.05.1998; advertiser's logo on front)
- The Empire Rochdale + Foster's Ice (until 31.7.98.)
- The Swan Hotel Bolton + Foster's Ice (until 31.7.98.)
- McDonald's (all participating Greater Manchester Restaurants: until 30.09.98.)
- Source: Vodka & Fruit Spring water (scented)
- McDonald's (all participating Greater Manchester Restaurants: until 30.11.98)
- Nemesis (Rochdale: Wednesday nights)
- National Blood Service / Organ donation

- Telewest Communications ("Get Connected To Cable")
- Desire Nightclub, Bolton (Wednesday, Thursday and Friday: until 30.04.99)
- Desire Nightclub, Bolton (Wednesday, Thursday and Saturday until 30.04.1999)
- subliminal advertising experiment (french connection uk)
- xse (french connection uk)
- new deal for lone parents

7 Day Tickets Available on the bus

This operator has a range of laminated cards for various tickets valid for seven days from the day of issue. At the beginning of the 12-month period of this survey, all Segment and Slice (but not the Commuter) cards had reference to "BIG ORANGE" and "Greater Manchester *f*" title on front. By the end of the survey period, all cards (except for the Horwich Commuter ticket and the Rochdale Segment) had become First Manchester prints.

The range of cards comprised: Weekly (this covers all the services of First Manchester); Oldham Segment; Rochdale Segment; Moston Slice; Bury Slice; Eccles Slice; Bolton Segment; Wigan Segment; 26/34 Commuter and Horwich Commuter. A new facility, so that the initial card was a First Manchester print was the Leigh Segment. This was introduced from 12 October 1998. [In summer 1998, the Oldham Segment appeared in a promotional/data collection version with a rouletted reply paid card which could be completed and returned to win one of 5 Oldham Segments each week. This version still carried the Greater Manchester *f* heading.]

A late change - from 28 March 1999 (on which date there was a general fares revision on First Manchester services) - was that the Rochdale Segment became available for use on First Pioneer services within the designated area and the Oldham Segment became available for use on First Pennine services. (For further details, see under these operators later in this publication).

Complimentary Vouchers

The company has a policy of issuing Complimentary Trip Vouchers to customers who have been inconvenienced. There are two versions of this: one for Gold Service and one for all other services.

(As an aside, it should be noted that "Gold Service" branding was applied increasingly during the survey period to quality service routes provided by new low floor/easy access vehicles operating on a frequent or very frequent basis. The only tickets to show this branding were the vouchers mentioned here.)

Vouchers comprise two halves vertically rouletted: one for the outward trip, the other for the return trip. These were Greater Manchester *f* prints at the beginning of the survey period, but First *f* Manchester prints subsequently appeared, those for Gold Service having "VALID UNTIL 30th APRIL 1999" along the bottom edge - the "normal" issue having no such limitation.

2815   £0.66 09FEB99 08:38

Thank you for travelling with
GreaterManchester
Issued subject to published conditions

Thank yo
Greater
Issued subj

5135   PERMIT R 5524 510 0608

Wayfarer II

1690   £0.65 02FEB99 07:29

Thank you for travelling with
First Manchester
Issued subject to published conditions

2057 ADULT S 51 54 0253

Eccles Slice

ECCLES Slice

2613   £6.00 16DEC98 07:56

Thank you for travelling wit
First Manchester
Issued subject to published conditi

Thank you for travelling with
First Manchester
Issued subject to published conditions

5921   WEEKLY   568 50 0647

First Manchester

Complimentary Trip Voucher

COMPLIMENTARY
RETURN TRIP VOUCHER

This voucher entitles the holder to a Complimentary Single Journey on any First Manchester Service.
Hand it to the driver who will tear it and return it to you. Then please retain it for inspection.

First
Manchester
No. 102552
Not negotiable

COMPLIMENTARY
OUTWARD TRIP VOUCHER

This voucher entitles the holder to a Complimentary Single Journey on any First Manchester Service.
Hand it to the driver who will tear it and return it to you. Then please retain it for inspection.

First
Manchester
No. 102552
Not negotiable

6   Stagecoach Manchester

This was the other company that had been part of Greater Manchester Buses Ltd. - becoming Greater Manchester Buses South Ltd. in September 1993. It was sold to its employees in March 1994, although Stagecoach Holdings had also expressed an interest in purchasing the company. The company (which traded as GMS Buses) did not remain in the hands of its employees for very long, as Stagecoach Holdings took it over in March 1996. The company remains Greater Manchester Buses South Ltd. but the trading name became Stagecoach Manchester from 18 March 1996. Since becoming a part of Stagecoach Holdings, the Magic Bus name has seen increasing usage by this company, and the dark blue-liveried vehicles could be seen on three major corridors out of Manchester City Centre: Oxford Road/Wilmslow Road; Stockport Road; and Hyde Road, during he survey period.

The company has its headquarters in Stockport and operational bases additionally at Princess Road and Hyde Road in Manchester and at Glossop.

On-vehicle ticketing utilised Wayfarer II ticket machines until their replacement by AES Prodata equipment during January 1999. Replacement of the Wayfarers took place progressively during that month, commencing with Charles Street, Stockport on the 11th, Daw Bank, Stockport on the 18th, Hyde Road and Glossop on the 25th and finally Princess Road on the 31st.

Leaflets explaining the new tickets were circulated to passengers to coincide with the introduction of the AES Prodata ticket machines and the key side of these leaflets was as illustrated below:

Stagecoach Manchester Wayfarer machine rolls
The rolls with Stagecoach Manchester title appeared with this title and Conditions in a variety of sizes during the survey period. The largest of these titles appeared consistently on the definitive (i.e. non-promotional) rolls. To combat an increasing problem with fraud the final printings also incorporated an ultra-violet (UV) logo that could not be seen with the naked eye.

Quite a variety of promotional Wayfarer rolls saw use with this company during the survey period:

- Kellogg's Nutri-Grain
- Littlewoods Restaurant (two separate rolls: until 30.05.1998)
- KFC (Heaton Chapel: until 12.07.98.)
- Radion ("This ticket smells Sunfresh!" - scented)
- McDonald's (all participating Greater Manchester restaurants: until 30.09.98.)
- Stockport & High Peak TEC (Jobs Fair at Quaffers, Bredbury on 13 Oct)
- McDonald's (all participating Greater Manchester restaurants: until 30.11.98.) [two different prints of roll with same offer]
- Granada Studios (up to and including 29/11/98.)
- National Blood Service / Organ donation
- Namco Station (The Trafford Centre: until 30.04.1999.)

Magic Bus Wayfarer machine rolls
The Magic Bus definitive rolls also appeared in versions firstly without a UV marker and then with a UV marker. There was a shade variation to the printed text between

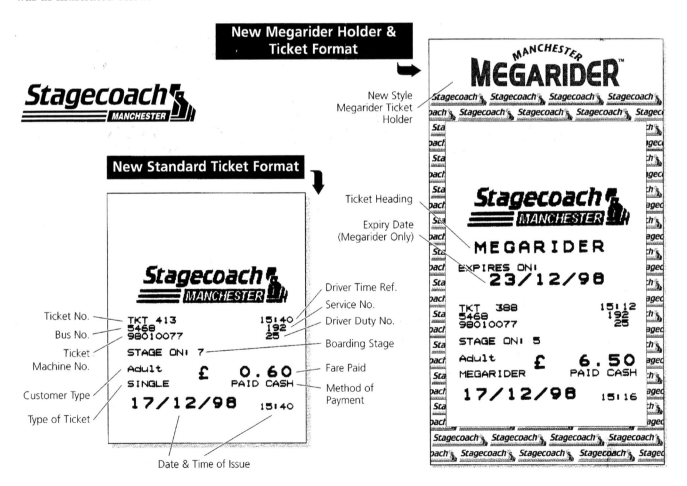

Wayfarer II

AES-Prodata

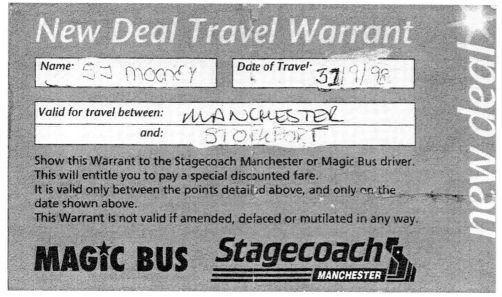

New Deal Travel Warrant

these two types, but otherwise there was no way of detecting these varieties.

A small number of promotions were seen on Magic Bus Wayfarers during the survey period:

- Central Trains (Manchester - Nottingham only £12.85 Return: fare valid until 17th December 1998.)
- Corona Extra (cartoons with Mexican hats seen from above and captions: "The town basketball team always got served at the bar first."/ "Carlos couldn't believe the size of Maria's feet." / "Pedro's Bar hosted a Mexican theme night." on different rolls)

AES ticket machine rolls
(Stagecoach Manchester and Magic Bus)

The AES Prodata machines issue tickets that are thermally printed onto heat-sensitive paper. There are ticket rolls for both Stagecoach Manchester and for Magic Bus, and these initially had title and Conditions down the centre of the front in pale blue. There is also an UV-sensitive repeat of Stagecoach down both sides of the two versions of the ticket roll. Unlike the Wayfarer rolls, it is just possible to discern this on the AES Prodata versions. The ticket machines print Stagecoach Manchester or Magic Bus at the top of the machine-printed text as appropriate.

A small number of promotions were featured on the AES Prodata rolls after the introduction of that equipment:

- Namco Station (The Trafford Centre: until 30.04.1999.)
- CALM (Campaign Against Living Miserably)
- new deal for lone parents
- Brannigans (The Albert Hall, Peter Street, Manchester: Sunday - Thursday until 29.04.99.)

Manchester MegaRiders

This company has only one 7-day ticket facility, the Manchester Megarider. Besides having validity on both Stagecoach Manchester and Magic Bus services, it is also issued by and valid on Stagecoach Ribble services in Greater Manchester.

A number of different versions of the card for this facility were used during the period under consideration:

a) With a solid blue background to the lower threequarters of the front - a design adapted from that previously used for Network 7 tickets
b) With revised graphics and an attached questionnaire survey on a business reply service card addressed to The TAS Partnership Ltd in Preston and 9.5 lines of Stagecoach logo repeats on the front
c) As b) but without the questionnaire and with 9.5 lines of

Stagecoach Supertram logo repeats on the front
d) As c) but now with 10.5 lines of Stagecoach Manchester repeats on the front
e) Vertical format cards for use with AES Prodata tickets
f) As e) but now with a square aperture cut into the laminated cover and backing sheet to improve the clarity of the details on the encapsulated ticket during its period of validity

The cost of buying a Manchester Megarider depended upon which service the purchase was made. From 3 January 1999, for example, the cost was £5.50 if purchased on Magic Bus services or on the 144 Campus Link service or £6.50 if purchased on any other Stagecoach Manchester service!

Complimentary Vouchers

Two types of complimentary vouchers were available for issue as part of the company's customer care policy during the survey period: one for an Adult DaySaver, the other for a Manchester Mega Rider. These had to be handed to the driver in exchange for an appropriate ticket.

Easy Ride tickets

Stagecoach Manchester in its various guises (also including Magic Bus and Campus Link - see above) is the major provider of services to the campuses of both The University of Manchester and Manchester Metropolitan University and also to the main student residential areas. It has therefore found it worthwhile to issue an "Easy Ride" term ticket valid on its vehicles. These tickets evolved in their frontal design over the twelve-month period. Tickets for the Spring Term 1998 (which were valid until the second week of April) were yellow; Summer Term were red; Autumn Term blue [see colour illustration of this one] whilst Spring Term 1999 were green. Available from September, and covering the entire academic year was what were described as "Three Term Easy Ride Tickets" available only from the sales agents at Manchester University and Manchester Metropolitan University. There were no special tickets! Purchasers had to collect the specific term's ticket from the agent at the start of each term.

New Deal

Finally, the New Deal initiative for the unemployed aged 25 or below led to operators being encouraged to give discounted travel to relevant individuals. Illustrated here is a New Deal Travel Warrant with Magic Bus and Stagecoach Manchester titles and available for travel between the stated points on the indicated date. There was also a New Deal Photopass - a yellow, laminated card conferring travel between stated points at the special fare of 20p.

Colour illustrations - clockwise from top

GMPTE - Wayfarer bus-train-Metrolink ticket, issued to a Group

Jim Stones - Concessionary 10 Journey Ticket

Rothwells Travel - St Joseph's School Concessionary Ticket

Stagecoach Ribble - Commutacard

System 1 Travel - County Bus & Train Saver

Warrington Borough Transport - Network Saver

South Trafford College - 20 Journey ticket

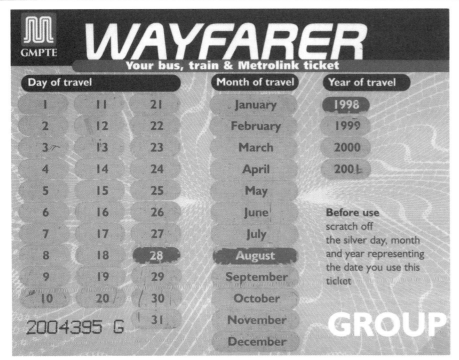

ROTHWELLS TRAVEL

1		6
2	**Tel: 01706 360066**	7
3	**Mobile: 0777 5771159**	8
4	*CONCESSIONARY TICKET*	9
5	**St. JOSEPH'S SCHOOL**	10

7 Supergem Travelcards / Day Tickets

In 1991 Greater Manchester Buses Ltd. introduced a range of Travelcards with the Supergem title. Despite the subdivision of the company in September 1993, the sale of the two companies thus formed to their employees in 1994 and the subsequent onward sale of both of these companies to major groups, the Supergem range of tickets has continued to be jointly promoted by the two companies. The tickets available during the period April 1998 to March 1999 comprised:

- Saver Plus - valid for 14 days for
  off-peak travel at 35p per journey   ticket serial A
- Student Term Saver   ticket serial B
- Adult 7 Day Saver   ticket serial C
- Adult 28 Day Saver   ticket serial D
- Adult 7 Day Off Peak Saver   ticket serial E
- Adult 14 Day Off Peak Saver   ticket serial F
- Teen 7 Day Saver   ticket serial G
- Concessionary 7 Day Saver   ticket serial H
- Commuter Season Saver   ticket serial J
- Commuter Annual Saver   ticket serial K
- Student Annual Saver

There used to be a separate print for the Student Annual Saver, but the stock was exhausted several years before this survey period and not replaced, the present writers never having seen an example. During the survey period, serial B Term Saver tickets were issued, suitably modified - though here again we have not seen an example.

The Supergem cards have passed through a succession of different prints. As they are on sale at a vast number of different outlets (Travel shops, Crown Post Offices, other Post Offices etc.) and in competition with the System 1 Travelcards and the operators' own on-bus issued facilities (in the case of the 7 Day tickets) some of them are issued only very slowly. It is therefore impossible to state categorically that earlier forms of some of the cards do not remain on issue. It is thus appropriate to list each successive type and indicate which of the tickets have had these (by serial letter):

Type 1 Printer: Orion
On back, reference in Condition 1 to "Greater Manchester Buses Limited's published Conditions....."
A [only]

Type 2 Printer: Bemrose
On back, reference in Condition 1 to "Greater

Manchester Buses Limited's published Conditions....."
A B C D E F [two varieties, with and without Off Peak availability details on back] G H J K

Type 3 Printer: Bemrose
On back, reference in Condition 1 to "Greater Manchester Buses published Conditions....."
A C E F G H

Type 4 Printer: Orion
On back, reference in Condition 1 to "Greater Manchester Buses Limited's published Conditions....."
A [only] [also known with security "threads" on back]

Type 5 Printer: Orion
On back reference in Condition 1 to "the Published Conditions of Greater Manchester Buses South Ltd. or Greater Manchester Buses North Ltd.,"
C D E F G H [cards E and F also known with security "threads" on back]

Type 6 As Type 4, but now with squared corners
A [only]

Type 7 As Type 5, but now with squared corners
C E F G H [card G also known without serial letter; card H also known with security "threads" on back]

The two companies also market a range of Supergem Day tickets, which are simply issued from the ticket machine, without any additional ticket holder. The categories are Adult, Family, Teen and Concession, and during the survey period they were sold at £2.80, £4.40, £2.25 and £1.10 respectively. It is clear that some purchasers of these tickets are confused as to which operators they are valid upon. They are valid **only** upon the buses of First Manchester and Stagecoach Manchester. They are not valid on Stagecoach Ribble services, nor on the services/buses of any other operator. Validity of Concession tickets is restricted to the GMPTE Concessionary area, but the other tickets have unrestricted validity with the exception of Night services, excursions and tours, service 144 Bradlegh to Haydock and service X1 south of Poynton.

Annual Commuter Saver

14-day Saver Plus

8 Arriva [serving ....]

Greater Manchester is characterised by having bus services provided by three of the major national bus groups, and locally Arriva has quite a presence.

The Arriva identity was introduced in early November 1997 to embrace all the operations of the former Cowie Group, the change of title being approved at an Extraordinary General Meeting of the shareholders. Bus operations were rebranded as **Arriva Passenger Services** from January 1998, and new limited company names (e.g. Arriva Manchester Ltd., Arriva North West Ltd, Arriva Cymru Ltd and Arriva Midlands North Ltd.) came into force on 2 April 1998.

Operations based <u>within</u> Greater Manchester comprise **Arriva Manchester Ltd.** with depots at Hulme Hall Road, Manchester (St. Andrews Square, Manchester after this was vacated from 21 February 1999) and Greeba Road, Wythenshawe. These are the depots that formerly housed the BeeLine and StarLine companies (the latter having been absorbed into the former and the airport fleet sold to Selwyn's Travel of Runcorn). [Hulme Hall Road also housed the vehicles taken over when Arriva purchased part of Timeline Travel Ltd. In Greater Manchester it was the operations based at the Trafford Park depot that were absorbed c. June 1998]. The former Wigan Bus operation was also part of BeeLine, but the depot had moved from Wigan out to Haydock (Yew Tree Trading Estate) in Merseyside in 1997.

The main management functions within Arriva Manchester Ltd. continue to be controlled by North Western (now **Arriva North West Ltd** [...serving the North West]), and a few services from this part of Arriva serve the western periphery of the county from depots in Skelmersdale and Warrington.

Arriva Cymru Ltd serves both Manchester Airport and Manchester Chorlton Street by service X3 from Chester. Finally, the former Stevenson's operation at Macclesfield became a part of **Arriva Midlands North Ltd** [...serving the North Midlands] with a Macclesfield - Manchester service.

Progressively during the year, the corporate Arriva roll for use in the Wayfarer equipment became commonplace, but the initial introduction of this came more quickly in some places than in others, so that ticket rolls from the previous company identities all saw use during the survey year. Indeed, the vehicles based at Greeba Road were still using up StarLine rolls in the Wayfarer 3 machines as late as October 1998, whilst some Hulme Hall Road vehicles were noted with the

Arriva rolls as early as mid April 1998. (It should be noted that the ex-StarLine machines show the date in double width characters, whilst the ex-BeeLine machines at Hulme Hall Road show the date in normal width characters.) The machines formerly used by Wigan Bus sometimes showed a WB prefix to the machine number. Wayfarer 3 equipment is also used at Macclesfield depot, and the jointly titled rolls for Midland Red North Ltd and Stevensons was still noted in use well into the autumn, although the first Arriva rolls were in use by early May. Arriva Manchester Ltd. and its predecessors only had one promotion on its ticket rolls during the year covered by this publication. This was for CALM (Campaign Against Living Miserably) in February 1999.

Arriva Manchester Ltd (and before that BeeLine and Star Line combined) has both a Day Ticket and a Weekly ticket valid on their services only. The Day Ticket @ £1.99 is not supplied with any sort of holder and the Weekly ticket (marketed as the "BeSt Weekly Ticket" in BeeLine days) is only supplied with a completely white laminated card. The issue description for these was "BLINE S A V E R - T K T" but this has now become "ARRIVA S A V E R - T K T". It was sold at £5.99 during the year in question.

Arriva Midlands North Ltd also have laminated cards for both the Five Rider and the Multi Rider facilities, and these can be issued for journeys (by that company only) within Greater Manchester or between Greater Manchester and points in Cheshire. Both cards were joint Midland Red/Stevensons prints at the start of the survey period, but an Arriva print of the Multi Rider was first noted before Christmas 1998. The cards are printed in blue and in orange respectively.

An "Explorer" day ticket was issued and valid on Arriva Cymru and Arriva serving the North Midlands services throughout the survey period. This was extended to Arriva serving the North West services from Monday 5 October 1998. Although not issued by Arriva Fox County Ltd., the ticket is also valid on this Arriva Group company's services, so that it now has a huge availability area for potential purchasers!

Finally, both portions of an Arriva serving the North West "Free Journey Voucher" are illustrated. This was one of five such vouchers received in January 1999 by a former colleague of one of the writers after he had written to the company about service reliability in the Altrincham area. (There had previously been a similar BeeLine version).

Wayfarer 3

G OF STAR LINE TRAVEL

ISSUED SUBJECT TO CONDITIONS & REGULATIONS OF STAR LINE TRAVEL

ISSUED SUBJECT

5989

519A 149 10:49 00AUG90 0663 ADULT SL

Travel
565 755557

Star Line Travel
Call our Helpline 0565 755557

St
Ca

856029

Stage 7 to ALTRINCHAM Interchange £1.10

Star Line Wayfarer 3

ARRIVA
serving the North West

FREE JOURNEY VOUCHER

Valid for one free journey on
any service operated by
ARRIVA North West

ISSUED SUBJECT TO THE CONDITIONS ON REVERSE
NOT VALID IF SEPARATED FROM TEAR-OFF PORTION BELOW

Date of issue 29-1-99   5567

ARRIVA
serving the North West   5567

FREE JOURNEY VOUCHER

DRIVER'S PORTION - NOT VALID FOR TRAVEL
Driver: Please complete details below, retain this portion of
the ticket and hand it back into the depot office

Date _____ Service _____ Journey _____

Free Travel Voucher

9 Other Operators based in Greater Manchester

The following is a list of 42 other operators and organisations based in Greater Manchester and providing services within the county (in some cases only school contract services) and [with one exception] issuing tickets during the 12 months survey period. Brief details of routes (or areas) where the operators could be encountered are given, together with ticketing details.

Ashall's Coaches
(James Andrew Ashall), Clayton, Manchester
This operator was very much in the news from April 1998, as he sought to introduce two Manchester City Tours using two (in the end it was only one) part-open top single-deck coaches. Double-deck open-toppers are prohibited from operating anywhere in central Manchester because of the live overhead wiring for Metrolink. The one vehicle that did appear some time after the inauguration of the tours was a conversion in the company's own workshops. The second vehicle did not appear, and a "conventional" vehicle always operated one of the tours. Tour operation commenced on 6 April 1998. Tour 1 covered City Centre Museums, Galleries and other attractions, whilst Tour 2 extended to include Old Trafford, Salford Quays and Salford Museums and Art Gallery.

Fares for Single Tour 1 or 2 were Adult £4.00, Senior Citizen £3.00, Child £1.00, and Unaccompanied Child £2.00. Combined tickets for both tours cost: Adult £7.00, Senior Citizen £5.00 and Child £2.00 (there was no combined rate for unaccompanied children).

Tickets, printed locally by the same company that produced the City Tour leaflets, were untitled - but nonetheless a very attractive range of twelve separate items, in a total of eight different colours. Twelve? Yes! Besides tickets for each of the above, there was also a Group ticket valid for Tour 1, 2 or Combined and for up to a maximum of 30 children and 3 adults - as illustrated. Very few of these were issued.

Indeed, so poor was the weather in Manchester in "summer" 1998, and so few the passengers, from 20 July the two tours were combined into one, lasting one and a half hours for which the fares were Adult £6.00, Senior Citizen £5.00, Child £2.00 and Unaccompanied Child £3.00. No additional ticket types were produced for this revamped tour. It continued - but still with disappointing loadings - until the first week of September.

Ashall's also provided vehicles for GMPTE school contract services in the Manchester, Oldham and Trafford areas. On these, the ticketing comprised Wayfarer IIs with plain white rolls.

Atherton Bus Company
(Paul Gareth Hughes), Westhoughton, Bolton
One of the (if not the) smallest local bus operations in Greater Manchester, this is an owner/driver company, with one bus on one service: the 592 from Shakerley to Bolton. Wayfarer II machine ATH541 being used for the issue of tickets, which have been on plain white roll.

B & D (Ronald Dootson), Leigh
Exclusively an operator of smaller-sized vehicles, B & D mainly operated routes in and around the town where it is based during the survey period. Almex A90 machines were introduced in early 1996, and although these have shown a number of text variations, during the period of this survey the tickets were invariably as here illustrated. Almex "A" equipment was in use prior to the introduction of the A90s. A few of these machines continued to see occasional usage during 1998/99.

A £2.00 Day Ticket valid without restriction on the buses of this operator was introduced in January 1999.

Bluebird Bus & Coach
(MTG, TA & M Dunstan), Middleton, Rochdale
This quality independent operates a fleet of about 30 vehicles on a variety of services, including (from 2 November 1998) a new City Centreline minibus service, replacing the service previously provided by Stagecoach Manchester. Other routes mainly link Manchester with Middleton and surrounding areas.

Wayfarer 3 equipment is used with titled rolls. These changed during summer 1998, to a version printed slightly more distinctively and in a darker blue than before.

Blue Bus & Coach Services Ltd., Horwich, Bolton
Another independent with a fleet of more than 30 vehicles, and a network of services mainly in the Bolton and Wigan areas.

One of the original second-hand Almex A's saw occasional use during he survey period. Otherwise it was Wayfarer 3 with titled tickets printed in bright blue, (see illustration).

Philip G Bradshaw, Heywood
A schools service is operated from Middleton to/from Hulme Grammar School in Oldham. An Almex "A" machine (without a title plate) is owned for the issue of tickets to the students who use this service.

R Bullock & Co (Transport) Ltd., Cheadle, Stockport
This operator (the first to place low-floored double-deckers into service in Manchester), and with a fleet of over 50 vehicles, operates on the south side of Manchester - along the Oxford road corridor, in the Stockport area and between Stockport and Altrincham. A very cheap fares policy operated during the survey period, both for NUS/Library Card holders on services along the Wilmslow road corridor, and for all passengers on some longer services (e.g. the 157 from Manchester (Piccadilly) - Woodford).

The company continued to use Wayfarer II equipment for ticket issue throughout the twelve month period, and with the original titled tickets (i.e. still showing a 061- (rather than 0161-) phone number).

Apart from these, the only other ticket that could be encountered was the ClipperCard-style 10 Journey ticket available for use by pupils at Cheadle Roman Catholic Primary School in Cheadle on the special service provided by Bullocks to the school.

Bu-Val
(Martin Bull), Smithybridge, Littleborough, Rochdale
Operates mainly in and around Rochdale. Ticketing changed during the year from Wayfarer II, which issued tickets on a variety of colours of plain roll to Wayfarer 3 (the thermally printing T120 version). This reflected the ticket system introduced by associated company, Universal Buses Ltd. right from the outset when that company commenced operations in September 1997. Tickets show "BVB" in an oval at the top of the printed data.

Checkmate Coaches
(Bernadette Poole), Mossley, Tameside
During the survey period, this small operator ran service 418 (Oldham - Chadderton - Lees Circular). Wayfarer II, 2850 was noted in use, issuing tickets on plain white roll. Also operated school contract services in the Oldham area during this period.

OAP   £00.34
From: 12 BIRD IT'H HAND
To: 1 KING STREET
F0034 Rt 652 Tm1330 D0001
09 Jul 98 Tck:5122 13:43
B&D COACHES
Adult Return Tickets
are available
for all journeys.

B&D
Almex A90

Bu-Val Buses
thermal Wayfarer 3

BVB

Route 438

3566   000000

Adult Single   £0.90

From:Daniel Fold

To   :Rochdale Bus Sta

At: 22:29 On:10/02/1999

GROUP TICKET
TOUR ①, 2 or COMBINED
MAX 30 CHILDREN and 3 ADULTS

THIS TICKET MUST BE PRODUCED
AS YOU BOARD THE VEHICLE

№ 000001

PRICE £ 25   VALID ON 4/6/98 ONLY

Ashall's Coaches
City Tour

Bullocks
Wayfarer II

`CK & Co. (Transport) LTD.   ISSUED SUBJECT TO CONDITIONS & REGULATIONS OF BULLOCK & Co. (Transport) LTD.   ISS`

3112   £20 15:51 05JUL98

BULLOCKS BUS
SERVICES
BUS INFO- 061 491 5525
COACH INFO- 061 428 5265

8471   5:1 £0.60 ADULT-SL

Blue Bus
Wayfarer 3

8112   Coach & Double Deck Bus Hire - Tel -: (01204) 668112   Coach & Double Deck

BLUE BUS   SAVE MONEY BUY A RETURN   BLUE

Travel is subject to standard conditions   Travel is subject

Chesters Coaches, Walkden, Salford
Schools contract services were operated in the Salford area during the survey period. Some years ago, this operator had introduced GMPTE-funded AES Datafare 2000 machines. During the survey period the writers were surprised to discover that this equipment was continuing to be used. Indeed, it was the only one of the operators in Greater Manchester to have had Datafare 2000 equipment and still be using it!

Courtesy Group (Eric Brook), Chadderton, Oldham
This operator provides a service to Hulme Grammar School, Oldham - and a number of services to Rishworth School, Rishworth, Calderdale. Single and Return tickets are issued from Wayfarer Saver machines on plain rolls. Up until July 1998, Courtesy also issued its own 10 Journey tickets for pupils at the two schools. These were of credit card dimensions, cards for Rishworth School being green print on white and gold print on dark blue whilst those for Hulme Grammar were gold print on red. They were printed by Self Style Specialist Printing of Oldham.

Dennis's Coaches
(Roy & Marjorie Cooper), Dukinfield, Tameside
Operates mostly in and around Ashton-under-Lyne and between that town and Manchester on an intensive service (216) in competition with Stagecoach Manchester. Although there have been titled tickets in the past, during the survey year the tickets issued from the company's Wayfarer II machines were on plain white rolls. A day ticket is issued for the company's own services. Prior to 14 November 1998 this was priced at £1.35; after 14 November it became £1.55.

Dunham Massey Shuttle (The National Trust),
Dunham Woodhouses, Altrincham, Trafford
A very interesting new service to The National Trust property at Dunham Park Hall that commenced on 11 April 1998 and supplementing the Arriva and Warrington Borough Transport Ltd joint service 38 (Warrington to Altrincham) that passes the main gate. The service was operated until 1 November 1998. There were five return journeys per day Monday to Saturday and seven journeys to and four journeys from Dunham on Sundays and Bank Holiday Mondays. An Ultimate machine loaded with three different titled tickets - as illustrated - was used for ticketing (now very much a "heritage ticket issuing system"!) The tickets comprised Adult (green), Concession (white) and Member (orange). The Countryside Commission financially supported the Shuttle Bus initiative.

Finglands Coachways Ltd., Rusholme, Manchester
This operator is a subsidiary of EYMS Group with headquarters in Kingston-upon-Hull. Many of the company's services operate along "the Wilmslow Road corridor" and pass the operator's depot and offices. Wayfarer IIs with titled rolls, printed in orange, were unchanged during the survey period (see illustration). The company's services are heavily focused upon the large student population to be found on the south side of Manchester City centre, and issues a number of period tickets to tempt potential customers onto their vehicles.

Two Student tickets that must be purchased in advance of use (and may be obtained either from the company's office in Rusholme or from Taylor's Newsagent in Fallowfield) are the Student Weekly and Student Term Ticket. The Student weekly cost £4.00 and valid on all of Finglands services. The Student Term ticket was varied in price depending upon the length of the term. Purchasers of both tickets must provide their Student Union Card number, which is entered on the ticket. A record is kept of this, and provides for the issue of a replacement ticket if the original is lost. There are two colours of Weekly ticket - orange and green and two colours of Term ticket - blue and mauve, and both types were issued in rotation during the survey period.

The company also issues on its vehicles two types of ticket valid for 7 days. Laminated cards are provided into which issued Wayfarer tickets must be placed. The first of these is called "FINGLANDS SELECTION", costs £4.00 and usage is restricted to services 41, 41X, 42, 42X, 48 and 140 (including night buses) - listed on the back of the cards. Blue with red print and pink with blue print cards used, although some drivers also found with green with red print cards listing in addition discontinued services 43 and 49. The second ticket is called "FINGLANDS WEEKLY" which costs £8.00 and is valid on all of the company's services including those from outlying areas (e.g. Halebarns, Whitefield, Marple and Bowdon to independent schools such as Manchester High School for Girls - close to the company's depot and office). Yellow and orange cards both with green print were used during the survey period. It is notable that both the Selection and Weekly tickets carry the exhortation "FOR USE **ONLY** BY THE PURCHASER". This would appear to be impossible to enforce!

First Pennine (operating from Rothesay Garage, Broadway, Dukinfield, Tameside - but a subsidiary of First PMT Ltd., Burslem, Staffs.)
Many of this company's services are focused upon Ashton-under-Lyne, and the Travel Office at the bus station is one of only two outlets for the purchase of the company's 7-Day Ticket (the other being the Travel Office at Stockport Bus Station). During the survey period, this ticket remained a pre-First Group print. Examples of both the earlier variety of this (with a holographic background to the operator title) and the subsequent type (with the operator title in red - as illustrated) were noted on issue. From 28 March 1999, availability of this ticket was extended to the services of First Manchester within Tameside and Stockport. Reciprocally, the First Manchester "Oldham Segment" ticket became available for use on First Pennine services, as did the First Manchester "Big Orange" Weekly: and this could also be purchased on First Pennine vehicles.

Wayfarer II equipment that had been acquired from the original Pennine Blue company continued in use and issued tickets on white rolls, plain on the front but with operator name, contact telephone number and Conditions printed on the back. During the survey period, the operator name shown on the tickets changed from "Pennine f" to "First Pennine f". First Pennine issues a Day Ticket valid only on its own services, and costing £2.50.

Glossopdale Bus Company
(David Whyatt), Dukinfield, Tameside
This company employed Wayfarer II ticket equipment on services mainly serving the south east of the Manchester conurbation. An agreement was entered into with Trent Motor Traction Co. Ltd. from 1 March 1998 (the "A6 Partnership") to jointly market their services between Newtown and Stockport and with Glossopdale Return tickets on route 361 being interavailable for use on Trent Airbus routes 198/199 and vice versa. The attractively printed ticket rolls used with the Wayfarer equipment (green print on white) had remained unchanged since first introduced (in 1997).

Glossopdale was absorbed by Stagecoach from 12 February 1999, but continued to operate as a separate subsidiary until the end of the survey period. It was understood that the company's operations would be merged into those of the Glossop depot of Stagecoach Manchester in April 1999.

By early March 1999, the Glossopdale-titled Wayfarer rolls had ceased to be used. Stagecoach Manchester-titled rolls (rendered obsolete by that company's introduction of AES Prodata equipment) had been introduced in replacement of these.

Goodwin's Coaches, Eccles, Salford
This company at one time used GMPTE-funded Datafare 2000

Bluebird Bus & Coach
Wayfarer 3

Courtesy Coaches
Hulme Grammar School
Concessionary Ticket

Finglands
Wayfarer II

Glossopdale Bus Co
Wayfarer II

Green Triangle
Wayfarer 3

ticket equipment, but Wayfarer 3's loaded with plain white rolls were in use on PTE contract routes to/from schools in Manchester, Salford and Trafford during the survey period.

Green Triangle Buses Ltd., Lostock, Bolton

This expansionist new operator first appeared in 1998 and has developed a network of routes in the Leigh/Wigan area. Wayfarer 3 ticket equipment was used from the outset, initially with plain white rolls but titled rolls had appeared by early September 1998.

Hayton's Coaches (Barry Hayton), Gorton, Manchester

Schools contract services were operated in the Manchester and Trafford areas. Some years ago, this operator was one of the group that had introduced GMPTE-funded AES Datafare 2000 machines. Now, however, ticketing is by Wayfarer II equipment issuing on plain white rolls.

Hulme Hall Coaches Ltd., Cheadle Hulme, Stockport

A fleet of around ten vehicles is run by this company, which is owned by Hulme Hall School, an 11 - 16 independent day school in Cheadle Hulme, and whose main purpose is to transport students to/from the school from a wide area of Greater Manchester and north Cheshire. The morning positioning journeys from Cheadle Hulme and the evening return runs to Cheadle Hulme are registered local bus services, and vehicles are equipped with Wayfarer II machines issuing tickets on plain white rolls to casual passengers.

For the students of Hulme Hall School, there is a Concessionary Bus Pass for those under 16 and a Bus Pass for those over 16. These Passes are home-produced by the company. Up to July 1998, the Concessionary version was yellow and from September 1998 green. The non-Concessionary version is always white. (Note that the school only caters for students up to year 11, and those who cease to be eligible for the concessionary Pass leave after the GCSE examinations each summer term).

Since September 1998, the company has been providing a contract service for another nearby independent school (Cheadle Hulme School). For this a folding green paper Bus Pass, including a space for the photo of the holder, has been issued.

Amongst the Conditions on the back of all of the various Bus Passes are the statements that "It entitles the holder to travel free on the journeys in accordance to the schedule issued" and "In certain circumstances detailed in the Code of Conduct, the pass may be retained by the official and will be returned to the parents." These are worthy of comment. Firstly, the parents of the students travelling with a Bus Pass pay for them in advance (and presumably receive a discount for so doing). Secondly, the return of a Bus Pass to the parents of a student will indicate that he/she has been poorly behaved. It is then likely that the student will have to be transported to/from school at additional expense to the parents and not on the bus! All of these various Bus Passes are laminated upon issue.

[Incidentally, there is one other Independent School within Greater Manchester - Bolton School - which has its own separate transport fleet (Bolton School Services Ltd.) In this instance, payment for students using the services is incorporated into the termly fees, and there are no tickets or Passes issued.]

JP Bus & Coach (P V Walsh), Middleton, Rochdale

A fleet of about 25 minibuses is operated on services mainly in and around the Middleton and Moston areas. Wayfarer II equipment continued in use for on-bus ticketing throughout the twelve month survey period. Two colours of titled roll were used over this period: yellow and gold. In addition, Merry Christmas rolls were used for a while in December.

K'Matt Coaches
(Brendan Newall), Failsworth, Manchester

Service 33 (Norden to/from Hulme Grammar School in Oldham) and service 22 (Shaw to/from St Josephs High School) are operated. Concessionary 10 Journey cards are issued for regular travellers. During the twelve-month period being surveyed, the cards originally featured black print on yellow. When a new supply was obtained ("enough to last a couple of years"), the colour of the cards was cream. Despite the two separate schools served, all of the cards refer to Hulme Grammar School!

A Mayne & Son Ltd., Clayton, Manchester

This old-established operator has a fleet of about 60 vehicles based at its Clayton depot on the east side of Manchester. Its primary services are focused upon the east and south east sector of the conurbation although some GMPTE contracts takes its vehicles to other parts of the area, particularly on a Sunday. Ticketing is provided by Wayfarer II equipment, and throughout the survey period the ticket rolls were unchanging: printed red on cream-coloured paper.

Perhaps surprisingly, no other tickets are issued by this operator for its own services.

Mecca Bingo - Breightmet, Bolton

A coach service from Heywood, Bury and Ainsworth to this entertainment emporium commenced from 25 March 1999, with a return fare of 50p. The service is provided on two evenings each week: Mondays and Thursdays. J M Whitehead of Rochdale provided the vehicle for this service. A member of the Mecca management collected the 50p return fare from each client as they boarded the coach to go home on both occasions during the survey period (25 and 29 March). No tickets were issued. However, as with other similar Mecca Bingo establishments elsewhere in Britain, tickets may be introduced in due course.

NB. There may well be other Bingo establishments in Greater Manchester that have coaches transporting clients on certain evenings - and with tickets issued - but the writers have no information to support or refute this assertion.

Midwest Coaches (Westbrook (Euro) Ltd.,) Salford

Services 692 [Castle Irwell - Salford University] and E69 [Altrincham - Alderley Edge (Tuesdays and Saturdays only)] were operated by this company throughout the survey period. Service 43 (Manchester Piccadilly - Northenden) was run for a short while in April 1998 whilst operation of service 244 Pendleton Shopping Centre - Chorlton Bus Station commenced on 25 March 1999. The company has a batch of Wayfarer II machines (numbered MID100 - 118) and prints these numbers on the issued tickets - which were on a mixture of plain white rolls and secondhand rolls ex Stuarts of Hyde during the survey period.

M R Travel (Mike Royds), Whitworth, Rochdale

This operator had a very limited presence in his base town during the survey period. Wayfarer II equipment is used for ticket issue, which is on plain white rolls. The ticket machines have a MR-prefix to the machine number that aids identification.

Olympia Coaches (J & S Lewis), Hindley, Wigan

GMPTE-contracted schools services were operated in the Bolton area during the survey period. Ticketing on these was by Wayfarer II issuing on to plain white rolls. The writers were told that machine numbers printed on the tickets have an "OLY" prefix.

Pioneer (J M Whitehead), Rochdale

This operator used Wayfarer II ticket equipment on a network of services mainly around the Rochdale area. Plain rolls had

HULME HALL COACHES LTD.

BUS PASS.

NAME..................................
Return journey to and from school.

....
NOT TRANSFERABLE   Valid to
CONDITIONS ON REVERSE.

Hulme Hall Coaches - School Bus Pass

1	*K' Matt Coaches*	6
2	**Tel: 0161 688 5817**	7
3		8
4	*CONCESSIONARY TICKET*	9
5	**HULME GRAMMAR SCHOOL**	10

K'Matt Coaches - Concessionary Ticket

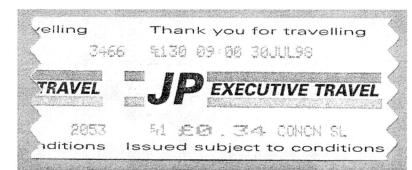

JP Executive
Wayfarer II

Mayne
Wayfarer II

First Pioneer
Wayfarer II

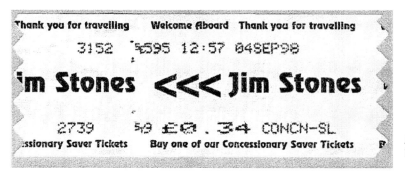

Jim Stones
Wayfarer II

been used, but rolls titled "PIONEER TRAVEL" on the back in large dark blue capitals (+ phone number and Coach Hire details) came into use in March/April 1998.

The company was sold to First Group in November 1998, and is now under the wing of First Manchester Ltd. However, it is being continued as a separate entity (First Pioneer Bus Ltd). In early February 1999, new titled rolls (this time with text on the front) came into use - still printed in the same dark blue of their predecessors. (see illustration).

A late development (from 28 March 1999) was that First Manchester "Big Orange" Weekly and "Rochdale Segment" tickets became available for use on First Pioneer services and these tickets could then also be purchased from First Pioneer drivers.

Premiershow Ltd. (Rothwells Super Travel), Heywood

A schools contract service was provided from Alkrington, Middleton and Heywood to/from Bury Grammar School, which has used an ex-Blackburn Borough Transport Ltd double-decker since September 1998. Single or Return tickets could be obtained on a daily basis and these being issued from a Wayfarer Saver (ex Wayfarer II) on plain white roll. However, there are also Concessionary Ten Journey tickets (gold print on red) and Concessionary Term tickets (gold print on dark blue) of credit card size for this service, and printed by Self Style Specialist Printing, Oldham (the same as for the similar Courtesy Coaches tickets, previously described).

One other school service was operated - to/from St. Joseph's School - a RC Primary school in Heywood. There are also Concessionary 10 Journey tickets - but black print on yellow - for this service. The school's PTA is responsible for selling the tickets and collecting in the proceeds. These tickets are also of credit card size and printed by Self Style Specialist Printing of Oldham.

All three tickets are titled "ROTHWELLS TRAVEL".

The company also has a coach booking office on the main street (Church Street) in Heywood, and has an agency for Ellen Smith. The Ellen Smith tickets are booklet type: top copy pink (for single/outward journeys), second copy yellow (for return journeys), third copy blue (which goes to Ellen Smith) fourth copy white (which is retained).

H & J Ramm, Sudden, Rochdale

This operator is also a major PCV dealership. During the school year 1998/99, just one contract service - in the Rochdale area - was operated. Previously, a service was also provided to Hopwood Hall College, Middleton from Rochdale.

Wayfarer II machines ex-Stagecoach Ribble are owned, and during the survey period "a miscellany of ticket rolls" was used for ticket issue (none titled for this operator)!

Ringway Minibus Hire

(M T & A and C I Walley), Altrincham, Trafford
Two GMPTE contract services are operated: 38 (between Warburton and Bowdon School) and 718 (between Oldfield Brow and St. Vincent Primary School). For these services the vehicles have Wayfarer II ticket machines and tickets are issued on plain white rolls.

The operator also runs Cheshire Bus service 110 between Wilmslow and St Benedict's Primary School, Handforth. On this run, an untitled secondhand Almex "A" machine is used.

South Trafford College, Timperley, Trafford

Not itself an operator of services, but for a number of years had subsidised a service to the college from the Macclesfield area via Wilmslow, Heald Green and Wythenshawe, and which was operated by Star Line Travel. This operator was taken over by Bee Line and then absorbed into Arriva

Manchester Ltd. Whether the College had already decided to discontinue subsidising this service or whether the new company required a subsidy larger than the college was prepared to pay is not known. Whatever the situation, the service ceased in July 1998.

Students paid 34p per journey, and bought 20 Journey tickets at £6.80. The ticket for this is included amongst the colour illustrations. (In earlier years, students had had the choice of buying 20 Journey or 40 Journey tickets.)

Springfield Coaches (William Trezise), Springfield, Wigan

Services, including ones branded as "Easyway" are focused upon Wigan. In the past, AES Datafare ticket machines had been used, and which printed the company's name. Now, however, Wayfarer II machines are used for ticket issue, these being loaded with plain white rolls. Some (but not all) of the Wayfarer machines print a SF prefix to the machine number on the tickets.

Jim Stones Coaches, Leigh, Wigan

Services are focused upon Leigh and ticketing is again the preserve of Wayfarer II equipment. Since their introduction, plain rolls had been used in these - often white, though other colours had been noted over the years. By September 1998, titled rolls had appeared - printed in dark blue. Text on the front included the suggestion "Buy one of our Concessionary Saver Tickets". These are dark blue cards, valid for 10 Journeys, and sold at a price, which undercuts the System 1Concessionary ClipperCard and which had been first introduced during 1998.

Jim Stones has also used "Seasons Greetings" Wayfarer ticket rolls during December, but it is not known if he did so in 1998.

Stotts Tours (Oldham) Ltd., Oldham

Having withdrawn from operating local bus services a few years ago, Stotts now concentrates on school contract services in the Oldham, Rochdale and Tameside areas. Vehicles are equipped with Wayfarer II machines which - as in the days of operating the local bus services - issue tickets on plain rolls.

Sureway Travel (Graham A Ing), Pemberton, Wigan

Some local bus work - service 623 Wigan Bus Station to Robin Park and service 644 Wrightington Hospital - Wigan (from 22 February 1999) - plus GMPTE school contracts - were operated during the survey period.

Sureway have Wayfarer II machines that issue tickets on plain white rolls. Tickets show an "SWT" prefix to the machine numbers.

Swans Coach Hire

(BG & JA Swindells), Chadderton, Oldham
A number of school contract services are operated, including some to/from Hulme Grammar School in Oldham. The students using these services purchase and use GMPTE Concessionary ClipperCards. No ticket machines are used, and pupils using Swans' vehicles on a casual basis just pay a cash fare to the driver for which no ticket is provided.

Timeline Travel Ltd., Leigh

This operator had quite an extensive (although thinly spread) network of routes across Greater Manchester (and into Merseyside and Cheshire), and quite a lot of GMPTE contract work was included in this.

The company used Wayfarer II equipment with titled rolls featuring text in orange - that failed to evolve into a type including a phoneONE day number (0942 682222 appearing on the rolls until the end).

The end came in two stages. In the first stage, the company's operations based on depots at Trafford Park and Lowton passed to Arriva Manchester Ltd and Arriva North West Ltd respectively, whilst operations based at Shifnal in Shropshire passed to Arriva Midlands North Ltd. The second stage came in October 1998 when the remainder of the company's operations in Greater Manchester - and operated from a depot in Gas Street, Bolton - were sold to First Group, and absorbed into First Manchester Ltd.

The company had had its own multi-journey ticket, the "Timeline Tentimer" offering eleven journeys for the price of ten - and obtainable on-bus. For this facility there was a laminated card, printed in orange and black on white. Very few were ever noted in use by the writers, and although the dimensions of the card comfortably took an inserted Wayfarer ticket, the specially ruled area to help position the inserted ticket was appropriate for an Almex issue! Almex machines had ceased to be used c.1992.

Universal Buses Ltd.,
Smithybridge, Littleborough, Rochdale

A new company that commenced operations around a clutch of GMPTE-tendered school services, mainly in the Stockport area plus journeys between Rochdale and Manchester, in September 1997 and utilising a fleet of new vehicles. Since then, there has been a gentle expansion of operations, mainly on the eastern side of the Manchester conurbation, and further new vehicles have been obtained.

Wayfarer 3 ticket machines (the thermally printing T120 version) have been used from the beginning. Initially the full company name was printed at the head of each ticket, but during the survey period the machines were reprogrammed to show "UBL" in an oval - fleet name style.

Vales Coaches (Manchester) Ltd., Cheetham, Salford
Vales operate a fleet of about 20 small-sized vehicles on an assortment of services that can scarcely be called a "network", from Farnworth in the west to Ashton-under-Lyne in the east. Although some of the services are commercially operated, many are GMPTE contracts.

Wayfarer II ticket equipment is used for ticket issue, and titled rolls with text in dark blue on white have remained unchanged in style since they were introduced in replacement of plain white rolls in late 1995.

Viking Coaches (Alan Warburton), Heywood, Rochdale
Several school contract services are operated, and vehicles are equipped with Wayfarer II machines. Tickets issued during the survey period have been on plain rolls. Both yellow and white, obtained from Preston Fare Collection Systems, have been used.

Thomas Williams, Mossley, Tameside
Service 838 to/from St Mary's RC Primary School in Marple Bridge has been operated during the survey period (schooldays only). Ticketing has comprised a Wayfarer II ticket machine issuing tickets on plain white rolls.

Universal Buses thermal Wayfarer 3

10 Operators based outside Greater Manchester and providing services to it/within it

J Abbott & Sons (Blackpool) Ltd., Blackpool
This operator has for very many years provided summer seasonal services from Manchester through to Blackpool and Fleetwood and during the survey period these ran from 2 April until 31 October. Travel can be pre-booked at a number of agencies, but a walk-on facility is also available. Irrespective of this, ticketing comprises the same booklet style tickets with different coupons for Single/Outward and Return journey legs.

ABC Travel
(D & M Garnett), Ainsdale, Southport, Merseyside
A major infrastructure development in Greater Manchester during the twelve months being considered by this publication was the opening of a major out-of-town shopping complex at Dumplington, adjacent to the M60 and Trafford Park and called "The Trafford Centre". Since it was opened in early September 1998, it has attracted an ever-increasing number of bus services from locations within Greater Manchester as well as from more distant places.

ABC Travel introduced a twice-daily (Monday to Saturday) service (X17) from Southport via Ormskirk and Skelmersdale to the Trafford Centre (and on to Manchester Chorlton Street) from 3 October 1998. The company uses Wayfarer 3 equipment and titled rolls (red print on white). The ticket illustrated was issued as a Return for the complete Southport (Eastbank Street Square) to Manchester (Chorlton Street) journey at £5.50 on Saturday 20 February 1999.

C & M Travel Ltd. (CMT Buses) of Aintree, Merseyside, acquired this operator in late February 1999 and a limited company (ABC Buses Ltd) was then formed, and based at Formby.

Blackburn Borough Transport Ltd.
Limited stop services X1 (Clitheroe to Manchester) and 702 (Clitheroe to Bury) were operated throughout the twelve-month period of our survey. The Manchester services terminated at Chorlton Street Bus & Coach station, the Bury service at the Bus/Metrolink Interchange.

The company utilises Wayfarer II ticket equipment and titled rolls featuring green print on white. A range of self-advertisements appears on the back of each ticket issued. The ticket illustrated was issued to one of the present writers on 9 January 1999 when a vehicle on the 702 service en route for Bury appeared at his local bus stop ahead of competing vehicles of Rossendale Transport and First Manchester. It will be noted that the ticket was issued as a £3.00 Day Saver (valid on all buses within Greater Manchester as part of the "Integrate" scheme - see previously). Towards the end of the survey period, this company used promotional rolls for "new deal for lone parents".

Blackburn Transport also issues a range of Rover Season tickets - for periods of one week, four weeks and 12 weeks and for three zones: Town, Town & Country and Network. Only the Network tickets are valid for travel into and in Greater Manchester. These tickets can be either office issues or (to anybody with a valid photocard) issued on the bus.

Eric Bowers (Coaches) Ltd., Chapel-en-le-Frith, Derbys.
Operates service 355 (Hayfield - Marple). Wayfarer 3 ticket equipment was introduced on this service in June 1998, tickets being issued on plain white rolls. Prior to this, a mixture of second-hand Setright and Almex "A" machines had been used for ticket issue, neither of which showed any specific reference to this operator.

Carriers Contract Services
(Martin K Carrier), Bretherton, Lancashire
This is the operator of service 326, between Wigan and Dalton via Roby Mill, which operated on a daily basis with one journey in each direction during the survey period. Extra journeys (on Tuesdays and Fridays only) were introduced from 18 January 1999, courtesy of subsidy from Lancashire County Council's £750,000 rural bus grant, and covering three years. Ticketing is from a secondhand Almex model "A" machine issuing tickets without an operator's title.

From 18 January until 6 March 1999, half price travel was made available to all passengers on this service (? the new journeys only) on the sections of route not covered by commercial bus services. Lancashire County Council concessionary pass holders were included in this offer.

Darwen Coach Services
(D R Russell), Darwen, Lancashire
This operator has run the Sunday service on route 535 (Blackburn - Bolton) - 4 journeys in each direction - since 28 April 1996.

The writers did not see this operator during the survey period, but a 1997 report in the Transport Ticket Society *Journal* showed Wayfarer Saver equipment issuing tickets on blank white rolls in use.

East Lancashire Motor Services
(J G Haydock), Langho, Blackburn
This operator has a range of services that link points within Greater Manchester to/from points in Lancashire:

X9   Hyde - Ashton - Oldham - Rochdale - Bury to Blackpool and Fleetwood (Tu, Th, S, Su: but only twice per week during the period December - March);

X15   Colne - Nelson - Burnley - Accrington - Oswaldtwistle - Darwen - Bolton (Th only);

X28   Hyde - Ashton - Oldham - Rochdale - Bury to Southport (F only);

X44   Blackburn - Bury (F only) [extended to The Trafford Centre when this opened in September 1998];

X85   Bury - Skipton (W only);

X87   Hyde - Ashton - Oldham - Rochdale - Howarth, Keighley and Skipton (W only).

Ticketing on these services comprises Wayfarer Saver equipment issuing on plain white rolls. There are no other types of tickets.

First Calderline
(services operated from depots in Todmorden and Halifax)
First Huddersfield
(service operated from Huddersfield depot)
Both of these operators, part of **Yorkshire Rider Ltd.,** run into the north east corner of Greater Manchester (to Rochdale and to Oldham, respectively). During the course of the survey period the Wayfarer II equipment used by both operators changed from issuing "definitive" tickets titled "CalderLine *f*" and "Kingfisher Huddersfield *f*" to "First *f* Calderline" and "First *f* Huddersfield" respectively. Both operators also had a range of special promotional ticket rolls, and these will have seen use on vehicles operating into Greater Manchester. First Huddersfield re-equipped with Wayfarer 3 from 28 March 1999.

It should be noted that the Rochdale Segment ticket is actually jointly titled and jointly issued by First Calderline and First Manchester, although during the survey period the original issue of this laminated card (with Calderline *f* and

ABC Buses Wayfarer 3

National Express Wayfarer 3

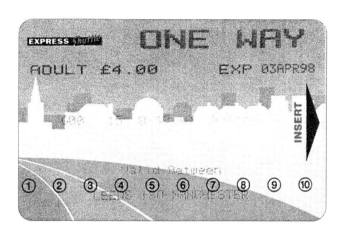

National Express Wayfarer MCV card

National Express ATB coupon stub

Lancashire Travel
Wayfarer II

Greater Manchester *f* titles) remained in use with both operators.

Lancashire Travel / MTL North
(Merseyside Transport Ltd.), Liverpool

The main services provided by this operator and permeating the Greater Manchester boundary are the 62 (St Helens - Wigan) and the 34 (St Helens - Leigh) although the 156 (St Helens - Ashton-in-Makerfield) also grazes the southwestern extremity!

Wayfarer II equipment continued to be used by this operator from the St Helens depot during the twelve-month period surveyed. Lancashire Travel-titled rolls, printed blue on white were generally used over this period, but MTL titled promotional tickets (printed brown on white) also appeared from time to time. In March 1999, new "definitive" Wayfarer rolls showing "MTL North" printed in blue and featuring a series of company advertisements for the SuperSaver range of tickets on the back appeared. The ticket illustrated shows a ticket found in Leigh just after the end of this publication's survey period!

MTL SuperSaver period tickets [with validity in All Areas or just in Area A (St Helens)] were also valid for travel throughout these services as were MTL DaySaver tickets.

National Express
Chorlton Street bus and coach station close to Piccadilly in central Manchester, is a major terminus/interchange point on the National Express network of services. Many of the services to/from Chorlton Street call at Manchester Airport, and a fare of £2.00 Single, £3.00 Day Return or £4.00 Period Return is charged between the Airport and Chorlton Street on these services.

National Express customers arriving in Manchester with ticket vouchers for the leg to the new Trafford Centre shopping mall (and which is **not** served by any National Express service), may use these on Stagecoach Manchester services 250/251. The voucher is surrendered in exchange for a Stagecoach Manchester £1.50 Return ticket. The Stagecoach driver hands in the voucher with his/her duty report slip and takings.

A very frequent "Express Shuttle" service operated between Liverpool and Leeds via Manchester during the survey period. Fares charged increased from 18 May 1998 and were then as follows*:

	One Way	Day Return	Period Return	10 Trip
Liverpool - Manchester	£3.50	£4.00	£6.00	£18
Leeds - Manchester	£4.50	£5.50	£8.00	£25

* reduced rates applied for children and Coach Card holders

Office issues for these tickets comprised magnetic cards. At the beginning of the survey period these were attractively designed and multicoloured and included a silhouette of an urban scene. During the course of the year much plainer cards superseded these, with front coloured pink and pre-printed matter in red. The tickets are issued through an office Wayfarer 3 system, and validated upon boarding the vehicle in a magnetic card validator (MCV). A problem with the 10 Trip tickets led to something of a backward step in technological terms when the magnetic cards were replaced by special laminated cards (headed "10 TRIP (logo) MULTIRIDE"), orange with black print - with a Wayfarer roll ticket inserted - around October 1998.

Tickets should be purchased from the booking office prior to travelling. However, if this is closed, Express Shuttle drivers can issue tickets through the Wayfarer 3 machines on the coaches. The ticket rolls used in the Wayfarer machines changed during the year from ones with blue print to ones

with red print and an advertisement on the back for 10 Trip Multiride tickets.

Season tickets can be issued for the Shuttle service - but only at offices, not on the vehicles. At Chorlton Street, these are magnetic cards which shows class "SEASON" printed top right upon issue and which are inserted into a completely plain laminate that is only slightly larger than the card. During the year, these cards underwent the change from multicoloured to plainer cards as for other issues.

The standard National Express ATB (Automated Ticket & Boarding Pass) computerised tickets covered many of the other National Express/Flightlink bookings at Chorlton Street, with issued tickets placed into an envelope.

To digress slightly, this ticketing system was initiated by IATA in 1987, with ATB format tickets having the following characteristics:
- "fanfold" packs of tickets 8" x 3¼"
- rounded corners
- a 'notch' at each end
- usually (but not always) an offset magnetic stripe on the reverse
- some are single coupon, whilst others (including National Express issues) have a detachable stub on the right-hand side

Whilst the ticket format is common, the originating computer system and hardware used to print the journey details (and hence the layout of the data on the ticket) varies according to the issuer. The system installed in the Chorlton Street travel office comprises one gateway machine (which runs the system), six workstations equipped with Olivetti screens and keyboards and three IER 557 ticket printing units (into which tickets from fanfold packs are fed through an aperture at the back, and ejected separately through a slot in the front). The system uses the EXTRA operating system and this runs "SMART" (Sales, Management, Administration, Reservation and Ticketing) software.

There are separate Flightlink ATB ticket issues, but these are only issued for telephone bookings by the central telephone reservations department. Flightlink issues at Chorlton Street have always been on standard National Express ATB ticket stock.

There are some facilities for which manual "airline style" booklet tickets continued to be issued during the survey period, including "Bargain Breaks". Such tickets are now also issued from the Inspectors Office when the booking office is closed. However, this was a late change during the period under consideration, as a Wayfarer I machine had been retained there. (This type of equipment had - in the past - been used in the main travel shop).

The various National Express Coachcards (Discount, Family and Lone Parent) can also be obtained at Chorlton Street and this office was also an agency for London Transport Passes and Travelcards, but this facility was discontinued from early January 1999.

Nip-on Transport Services
(Kenneth G Hatton), St Helens, Merseyside

This operator provided some vehicles on schools service 652 (St Edmund Arrowsmith RC High School to Hindley and Platt Bridge during the survey period, and also ran evening and Sunday journeys on service 156 (St Helens to Ashton-in-Makerfield). Ticketing provided by Wayfarer III equipment, issuing on plain white rolls.

Nova-Scotia Travel
(Andrew Gilligan & Brian Wilson), Winsford, Cheshire

This operator had a thin spread of services across a huge swathe of territory including Denbighshire, Flintshire,

Nova Scotia Travel
Wayfarer II

MTL North
Wayfarer II

Rossendale Transport
Wayfarer II

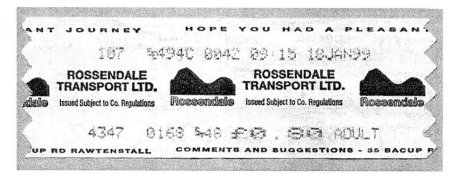

Cheshire and Greater Manchester during the twelve-month period of this survey. Ticketing is provided by Wayfarer II equipment and titled rolls are used, featuring text in maroon on white. The printed text appeared in two distinctly different sizes during the survey period.

Ringwood Luxury Coaches
(D T Brockbank), Staveley, Derbys.
This small operator took over the running of the X67 service (Chesterfield - Manchester) from **Henry Hulley & Son Ltd.,** of Baslow - and using a slightly modified route from that used by Hulley's - from 19 October 1998. A Wayfarer Saver machine provides the ticketing on this service, issuing tickets on plain white rolls. The issuer may be identified, however. In place of a "machine number", "RWOOD" is printed.

The writers did not encounter one of Hulley's vehicles on the X67 before their involvement with the service ceased, but it is understood that ticket issue comprised Wayfarer 3 using plain white rolls.

Rossendale Transport Ltd., Rawtenstall, Lancashire
This operator is an important provider of local bus services in the northern part of Greater Manchester - particularly to and around Bolton, Bury and Rochdale (in which town there is also a depot in addition to the main one at Rawtenstall, and having been acquired as part of the take-over of the Ellen Smith coaching operation).

Rossendale continued to use Wayfarer II ticket-issuing equipment - to which it converted over the Easter weekend in 1991 - throughout the twelve-month period of our survey. It should be noted that some Ellen Smith-liveried coaches also carry this equipment: and "Ellen Smith Tours" appears as a member of GMTL (see appendix) in their own right.

An interesting array of ticket stock was used over the survey period. This included:

- Red title and logo etc. on front; series of in-house advertisements on rear, printed in red
- Crimson title and logo etc. on front; series of in-house advertisements on rear, printed in blue
- Plain white roll; no text whatsoever
- Promotional roll by Image for Nemesis (used by Rochdale depot only)
- Seasons Greetings roll by Keith Edmondson
- Completely redesigned front, printed in green and including text along both upper and lower edges, and with a series of in-house advertisements on rear, printed in red

Ellen Smith vehicles used the current style of Rossendale ticket roll in their Wayfarer equipment.

"All Route Rossendale Rover" tickets are available for Adults (for weekly and monthly periods) and Children (aged 5 to 15 inclusive) (for weekly periods only). These have continued to be office-issued cards of credit card size, printed by Bemrose and with serial numbers preceded by "ARW", "ARM" and "ARC" respectively.

All Day and Off Peak Rossendale Day Rover tickets are also offered, and are purchased from the driver at the time of travel and are simply machine-issued tickets.

Stagecoach Burnley & Pendle (Burnley & Pendle
Transport Company Ltd.,) Burnley, Lancashire
Stagecoach Ribble (Ribble Motor Services Ltd.,) Preston
These two associated Stagecoach companies provide limited stop ("express") services into Manchester (Chorlton Street). Stagecoach Burnley & Pendle also operate on the 273 service between Burnley and Bolton, whilst Stagecoach Ribble operate Preston/Chorley/Bolton. In addition, Stagecoach Ribble has a depot in Bolton that operates locally in the Bolton, Bury, Salford and Eccles area.

Stagecoach Burnley & Pendle vehicles are equipped with Almex A90 ticket machines. During the survey period there have been changes to the machine-printed details and the ticket rolls.

The Almex A90s have successively shown the following details:

(i) Issued subject to / Company Regulations / Burnley & Pendle / Stagecoach Group

(ii) Thank you for travelling / Stagecoach / Burnley & Pendle / Please check your ticket

(iii) Thank you for travelling / Stagecoach / Please check your ticket

The ticket rolls noted over the survey period have shown:

(i) Repeats (in blue) of Stagecoach B&P plus Bus Enquiries phone number

(ii) As (i) but additionally with "express" between repeats of the company and bus enquiry details

(iii) Promotional ticket rolls were also been used.

Stagecoach Ribble have continued to use Wayfarer II ticket equipment during the survey period, though it had been announced that conversion to AES Prodata equipment would take place later in 1999. The ticket machines all have numbers in an RIBxxx series.

Various ticket rolls were noted in use during the survey period:

(i) Definitive rolls, with repeats of: Thank you for travelling / Stagecoach Ribble and "ISSUED SUBJECT TO PUBLISHED CONDITIONS THANK YOU FOR NOT SMOKING ON OUR VEHICLES " printed red on white

(ii) Definitive rolls for the limited stop services with repeats of: "Thank you for travelling / STAGECOACH express / Issued subject to published conditions" printed in red and blue on white

(iii) Promotional rolls. Bolton depot had two concurrent promotional rolls in January 1999 for Atlantis Nightclub with vouchers for Wednesday/ Thursday/ Friday and Wednesday/Thursday/Saturday nights respectively. No other promotional ticket rolls were noted in use at this depot during the survey period, but vehicles operating from Clitheroe, Chorley and Preston depots occasionally had promotional issues on vehicles operating into the county.

Pre-Stagecoach era Ribble office-issued season tickets ("Commutacards") continue to be issued for point-to-point bookings on services of both operators, and an example valid between Colne and the Trafford Centre (to which destination one X43 each hour was extended following its opening in September 1998) is illustrated. It will be noted that the Single fare from which the ticket price has been calculated is a mere £1.70!

A wide range of multi-journey issues is available from the drivers, for which laminated cards are carried to insert a Wayfarer or Almex A90 ticket: Day Explorer, Period Explorer and 12 Journey. prints of the laminated cards with reference only to Stagecoach Ribble were being superseded by the end of the survey period by prints with reference on the back to both companies. Manchester MegaRiders are also issued by the two companies and have availability on their services (in addition to the services of Stagecoach Manchester) but within Greater Manchester only.

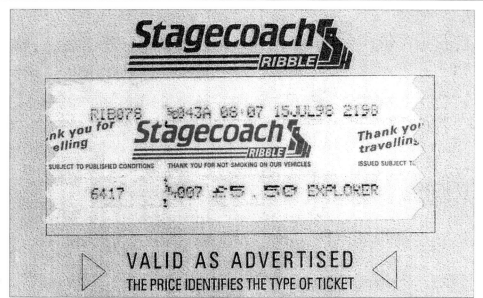

Stagecoach Ribble
Wayfarer II issued as Explorer

Stagecoach Burnley & Pendle - Almex A90

Trent Explorer

UK & North
Wayfarer Saver

Trent Motor Traction Co. Ltd., Heanor, Derbyshire

Services provided by this operator into Greater Manchester during the survey period comprised the limited stop "TransPeak" service from Nottingham to Manchester (Chorlton Street) via Derby, Belper, Matlock, Bakewell and Stockport and the 198/199 Buxton - Stockport - Manchester Airport "Airbus" services. The company entered into an agreement (the "A6 Partnership") with the Glossopdale Bus Company from 1 March 1998 to jointly market their services between Newtown and Stockport and with Glossopdale Return tickets on route 361 being interavailable for use on Trent Airbus routes 198/199 and vice versa.

Wayfarer II equipment remained in use throughout the survey period and issued tickets on the Trent Buses / Barton dual-titled "definitive" rolls printed red on white that have been unchanged for a number of years. Buxton depot was not allocated any promotional ticket rolls during the survey period; the writers are unsure whether any promotional rolls saw use on the TransPeak service during this time.

The company's own day "Explorer" ticket was valid on all Trent buses operating within Greater Manchester during the survey period. These could be office-issued (as illustrated) or on-bus issued (a Wayfarer machine ticket inserted into an Explorer laminated card, printed red and black on white and unchanged in design for several years). No other multi-journey tickets were offered by Trent on these services either within or outwith Greater Manchester.

UK & North Enterprises Ltd., Hadfield, Derbyshire

Until 22 February 1999 when daytime operation of the 99 (Manchester Piccadilly - Sale) commenced, this unusual operator had focused its operations along the Oxford Road/Wilmslow Road "student corridor" in Manchester, with services generally beginning at around 1600 hrs and continuing through the evening and on to "night service" operation.

The company issued tickets through Wayfarer Saver equipment throughout the survey period. Titled ticket rolls were used, with text printed in blue on white: a Keith Edmondson product.

In January 1999, the company moved to Gorton (which is *within* Greater Manchester). There is a new telephone number, but rolls in use at the end of March 1999 still showed the previous 01457 number.

Warrington BoroughTransport Ltd., Warrington

A number of services are operated to termini within the western side of Greater Manchester, including 19/419/588 Warrington - Leigh, 38 Warrington - Altrincham plus an extension of the 5 on an hourly basis (Monday - Saturday daytimes) beyond Warburton to The Trafford Centre introduced following the opening of that shopping mall in September 1998.

Wayfarer II equipment provided ticketing throughout the survey period. During this time, the company's "definitive" rolls changed from showing "*MidiLines MiniLines* (logo) Warrington Borough Transport" titles to ones showing only "(logo) Warrington Borough Transport" plus telephone number. A number of promotional ticket rolls were also in use during the survey period, and these will have been used on the services into Greater Manchester. These also latterly changed in style of title to mirror the definitive issues.

A Day Rover ticket is issued for unlimited travel - by the purchaser - on the day of issue. The ticket comprises a Wayfarer ticket encased in a laminated card - red, white and blue - (print code 01/98 noted in use throughout the survey period) and which have M and F punching blocks on the front. The cost of this ticket was £2.99 (adults) and £1.49 (children and senior citizens) during the survey period.

Warrington Borough Transport Ltd issues Weekly and Monthly Network tickets that are valid for travel on services that reach beyond the "town area" (and for which there are separate issues). These tickets are Bemrose prints, blue print on white card: as illustrated.

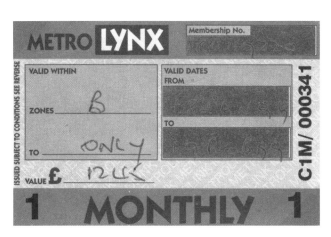

EAST LANCASHIRE RAILWAY

TEDDY BEAR SPECIALS

Free travel between any stations for 1 child and
Teddy on 'Teddy Bear Specials'.
Each child must be accompanied by a full fare paying adult.

This ticket also allows free entry
into Teddy Competition

0407

11   Railway Issued Tickets

No fewer than six Train Operating Companies (TOCs) provide services to/from and within Greater Manchester:

- Central Trains
- First North Western (formerly North Western Trains)
- Northern Spirit
- Virgin Cross Country
- Virgin West Coast
- Wales & West Railways

The main service provider, however, is First North Western and it is this company that is responsible for ticketing at all but three of the rail stations in Greater Manchester. The three exceptions are Manchester Piccadilly, Stockport and Wigan North Western. These three are important Inter City stations, and Virgin Trains handle ticketing arrangements.

Until 1996, rail fares within Greater Manchester were set by GMPTE, and the PTE therefore also carried a consequential revenue risk. The PTE withdrew from this arrangement as a result of what it regarded as inadequate reliability of a number of the local services. Now, following the privatisation of the TOCs, there is a strict formula governing basic (but *not* special offer) fare levels: essentially a "fares basket" arrangement. [We do not propose to elaborate upon this fairly complex concept in this publication!]

Many of the smaller local stations within Greater Manchester are unstaffed. However, a few of these are equipped with Almex AS88 passenger-operated ticket machines. Staffed stations are equipped with either APTIS or SPORTIS machines and some of these are additionally equipped with either Almex AS88 or Autelca B100 self-service installations. This information is summarised in Appendix 2. In relation to this, it should be noted that certain stations geographically in Derbyshire are included because they are regarded as part of the "Greater Manchester Rail Network" and the "Greater Manchester ticketing area" Note, however, that Disley and the two stations at New Mills are included ONLY in respect of Traincard sales and validity. SPORTIS issues from machines carried by conductors meet fares not paid before boarding the train. Passengers joining trains at locations where tickets could have been purchased should only be permitted to obtain non-discounted Single or Return tickets. However, passengers joining at unstaffed stations may purchase the full range of tickets available at the time of boarding (although it should be noted that SPORTIS cannot issue monthly tickets). The SPORTIS illustrated is an on-train issue from an unstaffed station (Flowery Field). It will be noted that the destination is shown as "MANCHESTER CTLZ".

This is "Manchester Central Zone" and all issues to Central Manchester stations from stations *within* the county should

show this (or the equivalent). Passengers are then able to avail themselves of the "Manchester Freeway" facility whereby onward travel into the heart of the city by Centreline bus, Metrolink (to/from Victoria, Piccadilly and G Mex stations to intermediate stations) or Stagecoach Manchester services 46/47 between Victoria Station and Albert Square is permitted without additional payment. This facility was available throughout the survey period. Tickets to Manchester from locations outwith Greater Manchester should show destination as "Manchester Stns" (or equivalent) and this does not then confer free onward travel into the city centre. Tickets issued for cross-city journeys should show route "METROLINK" where use of Metrolink across the city to Deansgate station, Piccadilly station or Victoria station *may* be required. (Outward half of APTIS ticket 69739 issued from Heald Green to Bolton shows this).

Special rail fares and tickets
- **Flat fares for accompanied children**
  These were valid 0930 onwards Mondays to Fridays and all day Saturday, Sunday and Bank Holiday, for children aged 5 to 15 inclusive and were priced at 40p single, 80p return irrespective of the type of ticket purchased by the adult. Up to four children could accompany each adult.

- **Elderly/Disabled fares**
  These were charged at 50% of the appropriate adult fare rounded down to the nearest 5p during the peak period, and at 40p per single journey during the off-peak period (and specifically on trains *scheduled* to depart after 0930 Monday - Friday.

- **Cheap evening return**
  (formerly known as "Happy Hour")
  Adults were allowed to purchase half price cheap day returns between 1830 and 2100 for travel between any stations in Greater Manchester and immediate surrounding areas (bounded by Macclesfield, Chelford, Plumley, Birchwood, Earlestown, Orrell, Burscough Bridge, Chorley, Blackburn, Rochdale, Greenfield, Hadfield, Chinley and Buxton. Manchester United Football Ground Halt was specifically *excluded*. Outward journeys could commence up to and including the first train after 2100, whilst return travel was by any train up to 0230 the following morning. There was no equivalent offer for children.

- **Greater Manchester Rail Ranger**
  This ticket allowed off-peak travel (until 0230 the next morning) throughout the Greater Manchester ticketing area at the following rates during the survey period:
  Until 23/5/98: £2.35 adults, £1.20 children
  From 24/5/98 - 2/1/99: £2.45 adults, £1.25 children
  From 3/1/99: £2.40 adults, £1.20 children
  A child issue from 9/1/99 is shown, issued on the wrong APTIS ticket form (should have been RSP 4599/5: One Day Ranger stock)

- **Greater Manchester Evening Ranger**
  This ticket allowed travel after 1830 until 0230 the next morning throughout the Greater Manchester ticketing area. Adult and Child issues were priced at the same rate of £1.25 until 2/1/99 and £1.20 thereafter. Both types of Ranger ticket were valid for travel on Metrolink services within the City Zone only.

- **Traincard**
  This is a rail Season Ticket valid on all rail services within the Greater Manchester ticketing area, and during the survey period could be purchased at staffed stations (Weekly, Monthly and Annual versions) or from

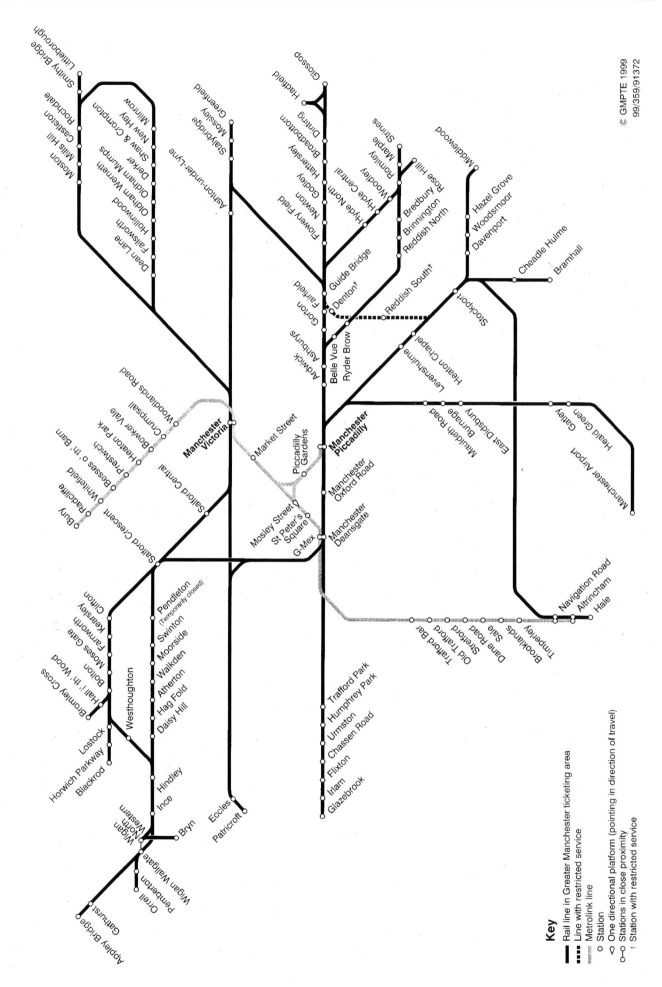

Key

	Rail line in Greater Manchester ticketing area
	Line with restricted service
	Metrolink line
○	Station
◇	One directional platform (pointing in direction of travel)
○-○	Stations in close proximity
†	Station with restricted service

Conductors on trains (Weekly only). A Monthly APTIS issue from Wigan Wallgate is illustrated, correctly issued on RSP4599/6 "Other Than Short Period Season" stock.

- **Point to Point Season Tickets**
  During the survey period, Greater Manchester Area Rail Season tickets provided not only unlimited travel between the two specific train stations named on the ticket, but at weekends and on Bank Holidays gave unlimited train travel throughout Greater Manchester. Traincard and Greater Manchester Season Ticket holders could avail themselves of the "Manchester Freeway" facility (see previously).

When fares within Greater Manchester were controlled by the PTE, there were APTIS cards for both the Traincard and Season Ticket facilities that included the GMPTE title. These cards have been phased out. However, rail-issued County Cards with the GMPTE title were still to be found during the survey year - as illustrated. The ticket illustrated is older BR4599/149 stock; some locations have had RSP4599/149 cards to this design. This stock was being superseded by a "System 1" print during the year, and a Bolton issue from November 1998 illustrates this (see colour pages). Illustrated here is a SPORTIS issue of a Seven Day GMPTE County Card from May 1998.

Through bookings to Metrolink stations are available from all stations within Greater Manchester, and at zonal rates (the train stations being arranged into three zones for this purpose). The illustration shows an APTIS issue from Manchester Airport for a through journey to Bury (in Metrolink Zone A: this being shown on the ticket). It is actually possible to book through to a Metrolink destination from any station in the country (and including on-train bookings). However, the writers have not seen such a ticket during their researches!

Finally, special mention must be made of Altrincham train and Metrolink station. This is the only direct interchange location between the two modes where ticketing facilities are provided by the railway booking office *in addition to tickets being available from the Metrolink ticket dispensers.* Consequently, APTIS tickets could be obtained during the survey period which were valid for pure Metrolink journeys: Singles, Returns and Metrolink Period tickets. Route is shown as "Metrolink Direct" as the Peak Return and Seven Day 4 Zone (correctly issued on RSP4599/1 card stock) illustrates. Note, however, that on Sundays during the survey period, passengers travelling to/from stations Altrincham/Navigation Road and Mouldsworth inclusive and wishing to travel to or via Manchester were permitted to do so by using Metrolink at no additional cost.

SPORTIS Single - Flowery Field- Manchester Central Zone

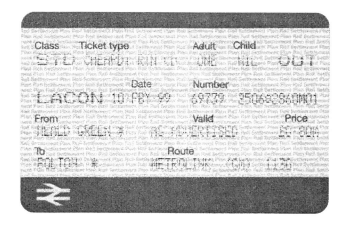

APTIS Cheap Day Return - Heald Green - Bolton

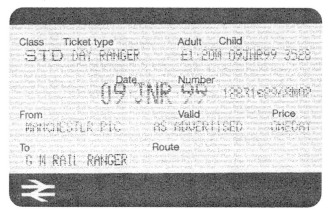

APTIS GMPTE Rail Ranger

APTIS GMPTE monthly Traincard

APTIS GMPTE 7 day County Card

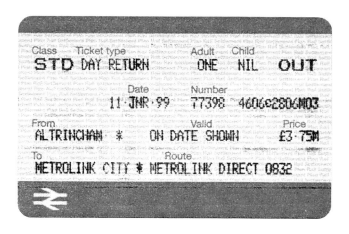

APTIS Day Return - Altrincham - City via Metrolink

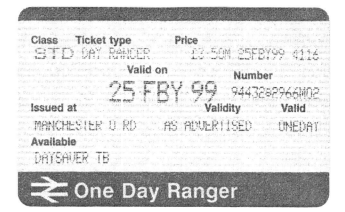

APTIS System 1 Concessionary Rail and Bus Day Saver

APTIS Day Single - Manchester Airport - Metrolink Zone A

SPORTIS 7 Day GMPTE County Card

APTIS 7 Day - Altrincham - City via Metrolink

12 Metrolink

"Metrolink" is the name given to the light rapid transit system for Greater Manchester. The first proposal for such a system was put forward by GMPTE in 1982, but it was not until 1988 that Parliamentary powers were obtained to start to convert the proposal into reality.

Phase 1 of Metrolink (Bury to Altrincham, and with a spur in central Manchester to Piccadilly Station) was opened in stages between April and July 1992 and officially opened by Her Majesty The Queen on Friday 17 July of that year. Construction had taken place between 1989 and 1992 and this phase covered a distance of 31 route kilometres, including 3.2 km of street running in the city centre of Manchester.

By any measure or criterion, Metrolink has proved to be an outstanding success: the fleet of 26 vehicles now carrying 14 million passengers per annum. There are plans for several extensions to the network. The first of these - Phase 2 - between Cornbrook (where a new station is being constructed) and Eccles commenced construction in July 1997, and is planned for opening in two stages. Phase 2a is planned to open to Broadway in autumn 1999, with Phase 2b opening to the Eccles terminus in spring 2000.

The initial operator of Metrolink services was Greater Manchester Metro Ltd (GMML), but operation passed to Serco Metrolink (a division of Serco Ltd.). in May 1997. This had an impact upon some aspects of ticketing, as will be noted later. The operator is based at Metrolink House adjacent to the works and depot, which is off Queen's Road a little over a mile north of Manchester City centre.

Passengers who do not have Metrolink period passes must purchase a ticket before travelling from one of the Thorn-EMI "Toll-point" machines: free standing machines located at each of the 25 stations*. (It was 26 stations until Sunday 9 August 1998, but the single platform station at High Street was closed from that date and a new island platform opened at Market Street the following day - usage of the original single platform at Market Street also being discontinued after the end of services on the 9th).

[* The situation is a little less straightforward at Altrincham, which also has a BR booking office. See the previous section above, dealing with "Railway-issued tickets".]

Ticket machines were located as follows during the latter part of the survey period (ticket machine number are given):

Bury	170 171 172
Radcliffe	150 151 152
Whitefield	130 131 132
Besses 'O T'Barn	110 111
Prestwich	090 091
Heaton Park	070 071
Bowker Vale	050 051
Crumpsall	030 031
Woodlands Road	010 011
Victoria	480 481 482 483 484
Market Street	440 441 460 461
Piccadilly Gardens	420 421 422 423
Piccadilly Station	400 401 402 403
Mosley Street	380 381
St Peters Square	360 361 362
G-Mex	340 341 342
Trafford Bar	300 301
Old Trafford	320 321 322
Stretford	720 721
Dane Road	680 681
Sale	700 701 702 703
Brooklands	660 661 662
Timperley	640 641
Navigation Road	620 621
Altrincham	600 601 602 603

The information printed by these machines onto the ticket stock comprises the following:

Top line: station of issue / fare paid / time / date
Bottom line: ticket type / ticket no / machine no / destination / zone of destination station

The "machine no" comprises four characters. The first two represents the station code, the third is the individual machine number whilst the fourth is one chosen completely at random, but which is the same at all stations on any particular day. It is not necessarily a number; "=, &, !, (and :" are amongst the characters that have been used.

Throughout the survey period, ticket stock has been white, with plain front and text on back in grey and aquamarine. Issued tickets are approximately 76mm x 46mm, and were as illustrated here.

The front door of the ticket vending machines (TVMs) is designed with a recessed panel so that the range of tickets issued can be changed (as happened when the "Integrate" range of day tickets became available from 27 September 1998 and again on 21 March 1999 when fares were revised and a new off-peak day ticket valid only on Metrolink, costing £3.00 and called "MetroMax" was introduced) or a banknote acceptor or credit card reader added without the need to install a completely new machine.

It is stressed that all passengers must have a valid ticket in their possession before travelling on a Metrolink vehicle. Passengers found not to be in possession of a valid ticket are liable to pay a Standard Fare (£20.00 since 1 February 1998). A white with black print ticket form as illustrated here was issued in such circumstances. It could also be issued as an Excess Fare ticket - or given as a complimentary ticket free of charge to passengers when there had been a service disruption, for instance. The ticket illustrated was issued on such an occasion. [It may be noted that when the operators of Metrolink was Greater Manchester Metro Ltd. there were separate Standard/Excess Fare Paid Receipt and Complimentary tickets whereas Serco have just this one form.]

A ticket form of similar size is issued upon prior request to Metrolink head office by group travel organisers. This ticket form is styled "METROLINK GROUP BOOKING" and is printed on white with black print.

A range of pre-purchased Period Passes is available to Metrolink customers, comprising:

ADULT: Metrolink Weekly, Monthly, Quarterly (not for one zone), Annual
YOUNG PERSON: MetroLynx Weekly, Monthly

Up until 20 March 1999, the Adult tickets could be purchased for combinations of one, two, three, four or all zones, whilst the MetroLynx tickets could be purchased for one, two, three or four zones. Here, purchasers of tickets for four zones received all zone availability. From the 21 March 1999 fares revision, the Adult all zone tickets were withdrawn, the four zone ticket then being extended in availability to cover all zones.

(For such tickets, the Metrolink network was divided into seven zones, as follows: Bury, Radcliffe and Whitefield - zone A; Besses 'O T'Barn, Prestwich and Heaton Park - zone B; Bowker Vale, Crumpsall and Woodlands Road - zone C; stations between Victoria and G Mex - City zone (zone D); Trafford Bar, Old Trafford and Stretford - zone E; Dane Road, Sale and Brooklands - zone F and Timperley, Navigation Road

MOSLEY STREET £1.00 11:51 09/05/98

FULL OFFPK RET 9020 3804 CITY CENTRE   D

Thorn-EMI Toll-point TVM ticket issued at Mosley Street

METROLINK. MI No.   SERIAL No. 1.6025

DATE: 2/2/99   TIME: OFF PK RET
LOC: OLD   FROM: ALT   TO: STPH
TITLE: MS
FORENAME(S)   S
SURNAME: DUTSON
ADDRESS: 384 OLDFIELD ROAD
                ALTRINCHAM

POST CODE: WA14 4QT TEL: —
ID: —   DOB: —

Delete as appropriate
STANDARD/EXCESS FARE TO PAY/PAID £   FOC
METHOD OF PAYMENT: N/A
PASSENGER SIGNATURE: Sandra M Dutson
REASON FOR ISSUE SERVICE DISRUPTION

INFORMATION/PASSENGER EXPLANATION
Please sign & date the ticket
before boarding a vehicle
on day of use.
                A. Colma

Excess Ticket form issued as a
complimentary ticket

Metrolink Travel Club photo-identity card issued to
one of the authors of this publication

and Altrincham - zone G. Very many period passes were sold under this system, but during the period covered by this publication, Metrolink was looking at the possibility of introducing point-to-point period tickets, or ones covering travel across a certain number of stations. Certainly the existing system was seen as unfair for those customers, for example, wishing to travel between adjacent stations, but which were in different zones.)

The tickets all feature black print plus a blue diagonally-printed security background on the front, orange data panels and coloured bands and boxes that are yellow (weekly), blue (monthly), crimson (quarterly) and dark grey (+ gold print) (annual). Conditions etc. are printed in black on white on the reverse of all the ticket types, and they also feature random security "threads" on this side. These tickets had completely replaced the types formerly issued by GMML, from May 1997. (The 1 zone MetroLynx ticket is shown amongst the coloured illustrations.)

Purchasers of period passes must first obtain a Metrolink Travel Club photo-identity card. These are unchanged from GMML days (the name of the operator of Metrolink not featuring amongst the five Conditions of Use on the back). [The card illustrated belongs to one of the authors of this publication!]

There are occasions when vast crowds of passengers have to be moved by Metrolink (e.g. when there is a football match at Manchester United's Old Trafford ground, a one day international cricket match at the Lancashire CCC Old Trafford ground or a major event at the Manchester Evening News [formerly Nynex] Arena above Victoria Station). The ticket vending machines could not cope quickly with payments and ticket issue, so mobile "ticket issuers" are drafted in to sell tickets at a flat rate of £1.00 at the station entrances. Tickets issued may be from one of six Almex machines or pre-printed Single Journey Special Event Tickets. The Almex machines were passed on to Serco by GMML and still print title

"GREATER MANCHESTER/ METRO LTD." Tickets are issued on white rolls. The Special Event Tickets are also ex-GMML stock. There were three values of these: 30p, £1.00 and £1.50. The 30p and £1.50 tickets are now issued with the fares shown amended to £1.00. The £1.50 ticket thus amended (and shown here) was found by one of the authors at the Piccadilly Metrolink station in October 1998. A late discovery about these tickets is that the £1.00 version at least is known with two different background colours to the "Event (where applicable)" box (yellow and red)!

Visitors to or guests of Serco Metrolink may be issued with a special Metrolink Visitor's Ticket, valid in all zones. This is printed in orange, aquamarine and shades of grey on the front (as illustrated) and on the back there are spaces for dates of validity and an authorising signature. The card features random security "threads" on this side.

The next year promises to be an interesting one for Metrolink, both in terms of the expanding operation and in terms of ticketing and fare collection. The system is being extended by the addition of Phase 2 between Cornbrook and Eccles, and due to be opened in two stages over the next twelve months as indicated earlier. This will add eleven new stations, including the one at Cornbrook, which will be the junction station between the Phase 1 and Phase 2 sections of line. Six new vehicles will be introduced and four of the existing fleet modified to run on the new line. New ticket vending machines by Cubic Transportation Systems (this company having taken over the transport ticket division of Thorn-EMI) will be installed at the new stations and all of the existing TVMs will be modified to sell a wider range of tickets - some of them being further modified to accept currency notes. There is the promise of Commemorative tickets to celebrate the opening of the two stages of the Eccles branch, and possibly a replacement of the zonal type of Period Pass. Who knows what may happen to the tickets issued from the vending machines.........?

Special Event Ticket

Visitor's Ticket

13   East Lancashire Railway

The East Lancashire Light Railway Co. Ltd. (trading as East Lancashire Railway) is a stretch of preserved ex British Rail standard gauge line between Bury (Bolton Street) and Rawtenstall. The company has its headquarters at Bolton Street in Bury, and a vast array of former British Rail stock has been preserved, and this is supplemented for special events by preserved engines visiting from other preservation sites.

The railway has three staffed stations: Bury, Ramsbottom and Rawtenstall and two unstaffed halts: Summerseat (between Bury and Ramsbottom) and Irwell Vale (between Ramsbottom and Rawtenstall). A regular service is operated on Saturdays, Sundays and Bank Holidays, and during the height of the summer (16 July to 27 August in 1999) there are also services on Fridays.

The railway is a very successful undertaking and is backed by a thriving Preservation Society, and it is planned to reopen the line between Bury (Bolton Street) and Heywood in the year 2000 (or soon after). The trackwork is complete, and includes a new and very steep crossing of the Metrolink line just south of Bury Interchange.

There is a vast array of "normal" tickets available on this railway, all of which are edmondson cards printed by Hackings of Church (near Accrington) with the exception of the Excess Travel Ticket. This is a paper ticket carried by roving travelling ticket inspectors and is mainly issued to passengers joining trains at the two unstaffed halts, Summerseat and Irwell Vale. It is light green with red print and illustrated here.

It is a very notable achievement that fares charged for travelling on this railway have remained unchanged since 1995.

Adult and Child fares between the stations are as follows:

RAWTENSTALL			
3.00 2.00 2.00 1.50	IRWELL VALE		
4.00 2.70 2.70 2.00	3.00 2.00 2.00 1.50	RAMSBOTTOM	
5.00 3.50 3.50 2.50	4.00 2.70 2.70 2.00	3.00 2.00 2.00 1.50	SUMMERSEAT
6.00 4.00 4.00 3 00	5.00 3.50 3.50 2.50	4.00 2.70 2.70 2.00	3.00 2.00 2.00 1.50	BURY
A/R A/S C/R C/S	A/R A/S C/R C/S	A/R A/S C/R C/S	A/R A/S C/R C/S

Concessionary return fares are available but not Concessionary single fares. Rates are £2.00 for return travel up to two stations, £3.00 for more than two stations. Platform tickets are available at the three staffed stations, priced at 50p (more on Special Event days) and there is also a Family ticket (two adults plus up to two children aged 5 - 15) issued for a full line return from any station at £16.00. Child fares apply to children aged 5 to 15 years inclusive, except on certain Special Event days when child fares are payable for children aged 3 - 15 years. Accompanied children below the payment age do not receive tickets, but instead are issued with small "publicity cards" (as illustrated).

In the following listing of edmondson card tickets, there are three standard colours in use: yellow for Returns, light blue for Singles and pink for Concessionary tickets. Other ticket colours are as noted individually.

There are a number of "universal tickets" (i.e. they are stocked at all three staffed stations [Bury and Rawtenstall only in the case of full line Returns] and are exactly the same stock at each location):

- Platform ticket - white
- Members' ticket - light green [ELRPS members are allowed three of these free tickets per year]
- Family ticket - white, with text in red and blue
- Discount ticket - green [issued to passengers in possession of a GMPTE Wayfarer ticket]
- Residents' ticket - green with red text [available to residents in Bury with a BL postcode, in Rossendale with a BB postcode and in Rochdale with an OL postcode; residents pay a fee, currently £3.00 per year, although this was under review at the time of writing; for this they receive a Residents Permit, printed red and black on white - see illustration - which allows personal half price travel on Saturdays]

At Bury, the additional edmondson cards are:
- Bury - Ramsbottom Single: Adult and Child (this ticket is green rather than light blue, and is still the original stock)
- Bury - Ramsbottom Return: Adult*, Child and Concession
- Bury - Rawtenstall Single: Adult and Child
- Bury - Rawtenstall Return: Adult, Child and Concession
- Bury - Summerseat Single: Adult and Child
- Bury - Summerseat Return: Adult and Child (there is no Concession ticket: the Bury - Ramsbottom ticket is sold)
- Bury - Irwell Vale Single: Adult and Child
- Bury - Irwell Vale Return: Adult and Child (there is no Concession ticket: the Bury - Rawtenstall ticket is sold)

At Ramsbottom, the additional edmondson cards are:
- Ramsbottom - Rawtenstall Single: Adult and Child
- Ramsbottom - Rawtenstall Return: Adult, Child* and Concession
- Ramsbottom - Irwell Vale Single: Adult and Child
- Ramsbottom - Irwell Vale Return: Adult and Child (there is no Concession ticket: the Ramsbottom - Rawtenstall ticket is sold)
- Ramsbottom - Summerseat Single: Adult* and Child
- Ramsbottom - Summerseat Return: Adult and Child (there is no Concession ticket)

NB Ramsbottom - Bury tickets are the same as Bury - Ramsbottom and it is this Concession ticket that is issued to passengers wishing to do the return trip to Summerseat

At Rawtenstall, the additional edmondson cards are:
- Rawtenstall - Irwell Vale Single: Adult and Child
- Rawtenstall - Irwell Vale Return: Adult and Child (there is no Concession ticket)
- Rawtenstall - Summerseat Single: Adult and Child
- Rawtenstall - Summerseat Return: Adult and Child (there is no Concession ticket)

NB Rawtenstall - Ramsbottom and Rawtenstall - Bury tickets are the same as Ramsbottom - Rawtenstall and Bury - Rawtenstall and it is these Concession tickets that are issued

EAST LANCASHIRE LIGHT RAILWAY COMPANY LIMITED

EXCESS* / TRAVEL TICKET

(*DELETE AS
APPLICABLE) Single* / Return

FROM   (Tick Once each side)   TO
. . . . .   Bury (Bolton St)   . . . . .
. . . . .   Summerseat   . . . . .
. . . . .   Ramsbottom   . . . . .
. . . . .   Irwell Vale   . . . . .
. . . . .   Rawtenstall   . . . . .

NUMBER OF PASSENGERS   Each   Total
. . . . Adult @   £. . . . . . .   £. . . . .
. . . . Child @   £. . . . . . .   £. . . . .
          TOTAL FARE   £. . . . .
Date . . . . Iss'd by

Issued subject to the Company's conditions and
notices. Valid day of issue for one journey only.

15443

Excess Ticket

Single

Complimentary

Return

Child Return

Residents Permit

Publicity Card

**Bolton Street Station, Bolton Street,
Bury, Greater Manchester
Telephone 0161-764 7790
0161 253 5111 (Tourist Information Centre)**

*Bury-Ramsbottom-Rawtenstall
Open every weekend and Bank Holidays.
Special events include Thomas the Tank,
Teddy Bear Picnic, Santa Specials*

Loco Works Admission

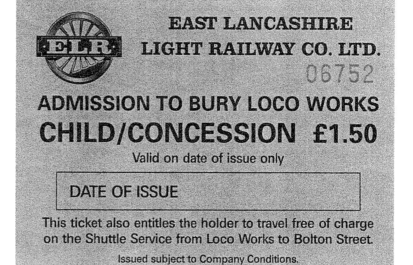

for return journeys to Irwell Vale and Summerseat respectively.

Thus, it will be noted that there are 44 different edmondson tickets available on this railway, and a small selection of these (marked *) is illustrated. With these is shown an edmondson-sized (but printed on much thinner card) Complimentary Ticket. These tickets provide for a free Return journey Bury - Ramsbottom - Rawtenstall. Various colours of these tickets were held in stock during the survey year, though it is understood that most of the tickets issued were (like the one illustrated) green. It should be noted that the Complimentary Tickets correctly show "ISSUED SUBJECT TO THE COMPANY'S CONDITIONS" (the edmondsons incorrectly show "COMPANIES"!)

A variety of different card tickets were also available during the twelve months of the survey period. Day Rover tickets were available for use on any operational day @ £15 adult, £10 child or member. The date of use is stamped on the reverse of these. These cards come in a number of colours: blue, red, yellow, orange, cream and green). Weekend Rovers were issued for use on any operational weekend, and these are grey cards costing £25 adult, £15 child or member.

On Steam Gala weekends (October 1998, January & February 1999) the Loco Works was open to the public and admission tickets (including travel on the shuttle service from the loco works to Bolton Street station at no extra charge) were issued. These are Adult green @ £2.50 and Child/Concession pale orange at £1.50 - although the actual rates charged were just £1.00 and 50p respectively. New tickets with these rates are in stock, but not issued during the survey period.

Special event weekends are normally very heavily patronised and for some of these there were special tickets.

- Thomas the Tank Engine Events. These were held on the early May Bank Holiday weekend (2 - 4 May 1998) and also the first weekend in October (3/4 October 1998). Normal tickets were available but these did not provide access to the special events. People wishing to travel and gain admission to all events could purchase special "Thomas The Tank Engine Event" tickets, as illustrated.

There were four types of these tickets: 1 Child (yellow plus red "C": see illustration), 1 Adult (yellow), 1 Concession (pink), and 2 Adults & up to 3 Children (white).

- Teddy Bear Picnic Event. This was held on August Bank Holiday Monday (31 August 1998). A feature of this day is that any child who has with them a teddy bear can travel completely free of charge. The special tickets were as illustrated [see colour section]: red (issued at Bury), yellow (issued at Ramsbottom) and green (issued at Rawtenstall). All other passengers purchase and receive standard tickets.

- Santa Specials. These were run on the four weekends before Christmas 1998, and special reservation tickets (210 x 75mm) completed in manuscript, light green for Saturdays and light pink for Sundays were issued. The special trains operated between Bury and Ramsbottom only and no through trains ran; passengers wishing to continue on to Rawtenstall or travelling from Rawtenstall travelled on a connecting service. Tickets for the Santa Specials cost £7.00 adults, £6.50 children over 3 years and £3.00 children less than 3 years (no seat guaranteed). The child fares included the cost of a present from Santa! To ensure appropriate presents were given the age and sex of each child had to be stated when pre-booking.

The railway also runs special dining trains, on which meals are served in Pullman style coaches. During the survey period these included Friday Evening Red Rose Diner Trains on 31 July, 4 September, 25 September, 16 October, 4 December 1998 and 19 March 1999 and Christmas Lunch Trains on Tuesday 15 - Friday 18 December 1998. Prices were £27.50 and £20.00 respectively. Tickets were not issued ,letters of confirmation of each booking being provided instead.

Finally, it must be recorded that Footplate Experience courses are run on a regular basis. There are vouchers available for purchase (that make ideal presents for friends and loved ones) and participants receive a Certificate of Achievement. Such courses were run regularly during the period covered by this publication.

Thomas the Tank Engine Event

14   Haigh Hall Country Park, Wigan M.D.C

There is quite an extensive 15" gauge railway in the grounds of Haigh Hall, operated by Wigan MDC Department of Leisure, that operated daily during the height of the summer in 1998 and at weekends either side of this.

A blue roll ticket was issued to cover the cost of a ride on the railway and during the survey period this was priced at 75p for all classes. It has previously been reported in the *Journal of the Transport Ticket Society* that the tickets are sold by the train guard prior to the commencement of the ride ("journey") and that travellers may retain their tickets. This arrangement persisted during 1998.

There was previously a road train operating in the park, but this had been discontinued prior to 1998.

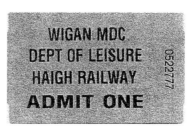

15   Heaton Park Tramway

This Tramway is owned and operated by the Manchester Transport Museum Society, and was officially opened to the public in March 1980. The trams run on a stretch of track that was initially tramway sidings laid in Heaton Park in 1905 by Manchester Corporation Tramways. The line has twice been extended since 1980 and now runs from Lakeside via the depot to the Middleton Road main entrance of the park, close to the M60. The depot/museum comprises a building originally built in 1906 as a large tramway shelter to accommodate 2000 people. It was converted to house a maximum of three single deck trams. The building also houses a small shop selling books and souvenirs. During the survey period, the two trams permanently based at the tramway operated services: Manchester 765 and Hull 96. The services ran on Sundays through to 11 October 1998

and also on Wednesdays in June and July. As a prelude to the 1999 season, trams were operated over the weekend of 27/28 March in connection with the celebration of the 50th anniversary of the last Manchester tram.

The fare structure on the line in 1998 was Adult single 50p, Child single 20p, Family (up to 4 children) £1.20, Adult all day ticket £1.20 and Child all day ticket 40p. The range of tickets for these during the survey period comprised white, orange*, magenta and green (with MA overprinted) punch tickets with "HENRY BOOTH LTD" imprint and green (with MC overprinted) punch ticket with "GNP-BOOTH LTD" imprint of an earlier style. An assortment of ticket punches is available for the conductors to use. [* illustrated in the colour section.]

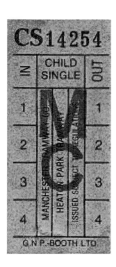

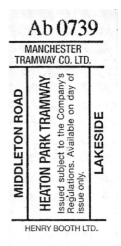

16 Conclusion

The foregoing should have given you, the reader, a clear view of just how interesting it was from a ticketing and fare collection perspective to have been a resident in "Greater Manchester" during the twelve month period covered by this publication. Certainly, we have rarely been busier keeping pace with all the new developments - and that would still have been the case even if we not been preparing to write the words contained herein.

Our efforts were made all the more enjoyable and productive thanks to the many helpful people to whom we addressed queries. Howard Armstrong, Roger Atkinson, Derek Bowes, Chris Bowles, Mark Brook, Lew Brown, Caroline Buckley, Les Burton, Tony Cavanagh, Paul Clear, Andy Coward, Michael Dunstan, Tom Dunstan, Sandra Dutson, Neil Ellis, Moira Fry, Mike Georgiou, Jack Hampson, Mike Hill, Keith Howcroft, Gareth Hughes, Jim Hulme, Colin Kennington, Bob Longworth, Stuart Murray, Lynn Ribchester, Ian Robertson, Dave Rowbotham, Les Runnett, Ken Savage, Robin Sherlock, Janet Spender, Stuart Stones, Roger Tripp, Andy Trow, Roy Walker, Mike Walley and Steve Wurr are amongst the very many individuals to whom we would like to express our gratitude, and all provided details to help us to piece together "the jigsaw".

Any errors that may be found in the previous pages are entirely ours, for we are but human beings!

Brian Hughes & Paul Smith, July 1999

Appendix 1 - Bus Operator members of GMTL as at 3 November 1998

Arriva (Manchester)
Arriva (Midlands North)
Arriva (North West)
Ashall's Coaches
Atherton Bus Company
Bellairs and Dootson
Blackburn Borough Transport
Blue Bus & Coach Services
Bluebird Bus & Coach
Burnley & Pendle Transport
R.Bullock & Co
Bu-Val
Checkmate Coaches
Chesterfield Transport*
Chesters Coaches
Courtesy Coaches Limited
Darwen Coach Services
Dennis's Coaches
Ellen Smith Tours
Eric W. Bowers Coaches
Finglands Coachways
First Calderline
First Manchester
First Pennine
Glossopdale Bus Company
Goodwins Coaches
Green Triangle Buses

Hartshead Travel**
Haytons Coaches
Henry Hulley & Sons
Houston Ramm
Hulme Hall Coaches
JP Travel
A. Mayne & Son
MR Travel
MTL Trust Holdings
Nova Scotia Travel
Olympia Travel
Reliance Travel
Rossendale Transport
Sports Tours (Pioneer)
Springfield Coachways
Stagecoach Ribble
Stagecoach Manchester
Jim Stones Coaches
Stotts Tours
Swans Coaches
Trent Motor Traction
UK & North Enterprises
Universal Buses
Vales Coaches Manchester
Viking Coaches
Warrington Borough Transport

Notes

* This is Chesterfield Transport (1989) Ltd t/a Stagecoach East Midland

** This is James Pemberton t/a Hartshead Luxury Travel, Mossley. This operator continues as a member of System 1 Travel, though we were told that they have not operated any local bus services "for several years"

NB: all of the stations listed are included in the "Greater Manchester Ticketing Area".

Station	A	S	P	Q	U
ALTRINCHAM	X				
APPLEY BRIDGE					X
ARDWICK					X
ASHBURYS					X
ASHTON-UNDER-LYNE		X			
ATHERTON		X			
BELLE VUE					X
BLACKROD					X
BOLTON	X		X		
BRAMHALL	X				
BREDBURY		X			
BRINNINGTON		X			
BROADBOTTOM		X			
BROMLEY CROSS		X			
BRYN					X
BURNAGE		X			
CASTLETON					X
CHASSEN ROAD		X	X		
CHEADLE HULME	X				
CLIFTON					X
DAISY HILL		X			
DAVENPORT		X			
DEAN LANE					X
DENTON					X
DERKER			X		X
DINTING		X			
DISLEY		X(T)			
EAST DIDSBURY		X			
ECCLES		X			
FAILSWORTH			X		X
FAIRFIELD					X
FARNWORTH		X			
FLIXTON		X	X		
FLOWERY FIELD					X
GATHURST					X
GATLEY		X			
GLAZEBROOK		X			
GLOSSOP	X				
GODLEY			X		X
GORTON		X			
GREENFIELD		X			
GUIDE BRIDGE	X				
HADFIELD		X			
HAG FOLD		X			
HALE		X			
HALL I' TH' WOOD					X
HATTERSLEY		X			
HAZEL GROVE	X		X		
HEALD GREEN	X		X		
HEATON CHAPEL	X				
HINDLEY		X			
HOLLINWOOD					X
HUMPHREY PARK					X
HYDE CENTRAL			X		X

Station	A	S	P	Q	U
HYDE NORTH					X
INCE					X
IRLAM					X
KEARSLEY	X				
LEVENSHULME		X			
LITTLEBOROUGH					X
LOSTOCK		X			
MANCHESTER AIRPORT	X			X	
MANCHESTER DEANSGATE		X		X	
MANCHESTER OXFORD RD	X			X	
MANCHESTER PICCADILLY	X			X	
MANCHESTER VICTORIA		X		X	
MARPLE	X				
MAULDETH ROAD		X			
MIDDLEWOOD					X
MILLS HILL			X		X
MILNROW					X
MOORSIDE		X			
MOSES GATE					X
MOSSLEY		X			
MOSTON					X
NAVIGATION ROAD			X		X
NEW HEY			X		X
NEW MILLS CENTRAL		X(T)			
NEW MILLS NEWTOWN		X(T)			
NEWTON FOR HYDE	X				
OLDHAM MUMPS	X				
OLDHAM WERNETH		X			X
ORRELL					X
PATRICROFT					X
PEMBERTON					X
REDDISH NORTH		X			
REDDISH SOUTH					X
ROCHDALE	X			X*	
ROMILEY	X				
ROSE HILL		X			
RYDER BROW					X
SALFORD CENTRAL		X			
SALFORD CRESCENT	X				
SHAW & CROMPTON		X	X		
SMITHY BRIDGE					X
STALYBRIDGE	X				
STOCKPORT	X			X	
STRINES					X
SWINTON		X			
TRAFFORD PARK					X
URMSTON	X				
WALKDEN		X			
WESTHOUGHTON					X
WIGAN NORTH WESTERN	X				
WIGAN WALLGATE	X			X	
WOODLEY					X
WOODSMOOR		X	X		

KEY
A = APTIS
S = SPORTIS
P = ALMEX AS88
Q = AUTELCA B100 (* TO MAY 1998 ONLY)
U = UNSTAFFED
T = TRAINCARD ONLY

Only three stations on the Greater Manchester rail network are not managed by First North Western: Manchester Piccadilly, Stockport and Wigan North Western.

Other Publications